THE FRESH GUIDE
ST. PETER

Fresh Air Publications

RUSSIA

ACKNOWLEDGEMENTS

The following people bear responsibility for this book:

Written by **Ben Lehrer**
Edited by **Kevin Penrose**
Copy edited by **Anne Robinson**
Research contributions by **Marina Shatrova**, **Anja Shaikevich** and **Luba Stepanova**.
Text contributions by **Nick Selby**
Illustrations by **Tatyana Paruk** and **Roman Savichev**
Maps supplied by **Katya Kachurina** and **Olga Manelis**
Cover photo supplied by **Anatoly Medvednikov**
Published by **Fresh Air Publications**.

Special thanks to:

Monster, Steve, Oleg Kazbekovich, Kolya, Lena, Julia, Asher, Frankie, Ulrike, Emir, Dan Crosby, Valentina Borisovna, Vika, Natasha, Irina, Sasha (*peredast*), Vova, Mel, Galina, Olga and Natasha, Charles, Katya, La, Kirill, The Brown Clown, Helen, Alla Borisovna, Tatiana Bulenkova, Maggie, Sasha Lobanov, Sasha Zhuravlev, Pirjo, and Pepe Lopez.

Comments, feedback, suggestions, inquiries and hate mail are encouraged. Please address correspondence to P.O. Box 163, 197101 St. Petersburg, Russia.

Contents

INTRODUCTION

All Petersburg is an endless avenue leading on to infinity.
Beyond Petersburg there is nothing.
- Andrei Bely

S T. PETERSBURG IS A CITY of deep contradictions. It is both beautiful and filthy, progressive and stagnant, Eastern and Western; it is utterly confusing and in the process of such rapid and all-encompassing transformation that it sometimes seems like nobody really knows exactly what is going on. There is more to Petersburg than meets the eye; despite its European appearance (the center being mostly designed and built by leading European architects) it is most definitely not a Western city. For behind the European façades and European-style waterways, lies a deeply wracked yet resilient Russian soul that sets this city apart from any other place in the world.

As with tourism everywhere in this country, you'll need to be flexible and patient. The State-run Intourist monopoly dominated the scene for years, herding tourists from sight to sight making sure they understood the proper ideological meaning of every one of them and all the while keeping track of their movements within the country. Occasionally they even provided guests with comforts and amenities, though this was probably an oversight. With the breakup of the monopoly and the gradual development of a competitive market, the tourist scene has improved dramatically. Still, Rome was not built in a day, and it wasn't built in Russia, so don't be shocked if you run into poor service, delays, mysterious cancellations, frustrating procedures and disorganization. If you accept the inevitable confusion and problems with a sense of humor and with the confident knowledge that in a few years' time St. Petersburg will be as cushy a tourist city as, say, Beirut, your visit should be very enjoyable.

ORIENTATION

St. Petersburg is located at the mouth of the Neva River which flows east from Lake Ladoga into the Gulf of Finland. Home to over five million people, Petersburg lies across more than forty islands created by the branches and forks of the Neva river. Finland is 175 kilometers (110 miles) to the northwest, Estonia 150 kilometers (93 miles) to the southwest and Moscow 550 kilometers (340 miles) to the south.

St. Petersburg is not all that far from the Arctic Circle. This means long, harsh winters with average daytime temperatures of -5 to -10°C (14 to 23°F) where the sun spends a few hazy hours above the horizon before disappearing for the next 18 hours. The flip side of this is the fantastic **white nights** between June 11 and July 1 when there is a brief spate of dusk at around 3 in the morning with light for the rest of the day. Locals wander about in a zombie-like daze at this time, partly out of the sheer wonder of the light in the wee hours and partly from the never-ending partying that goes on during this time of year. The best time to visit Petersburg is the period between May 1 and October 31. Spring comes late, with snowfall common through April and only in May do trees start coming to life again. Autumn is absolutely beautiful, with deciduous trees shedding their colors in the beginning of October.

St. Petersburg is divided into sixteen administrative regions. Down the middle of the city runs **Nevsky Prospekt**, Petersburg's central nervous system. Nevsky begins at the Admiralty and ends at the Alexander Nevsky Monastery and is the home of shops, movie theaters, chic restaurants, fancy hotels and a never-ending tidal wave of pedestrian traffic often harder to navigate than a cavalry charge. Northwest of the Admiralty is Vasilievsky Island, the largest of Petersburg's islands and one of the city's oldest regions. East of Vasilievsky is the Petrograd Side, home of the Peter and Paul Fortress. The Vyborg Side is to the east and north of the Petrograd Side and is home to many of the city's newer regions.

WHAT'S IT LIKE?

The Political Situation

The good old days when the government of workers', peasants' and soldiers' deputies operated in perfect harmony with the toiling masses have come to an end. The Communist Party has splintered into three groups. The first group has re-entered politics as born-again democrats, the second uses its connections and patronage networks for business purposes, and the third berates the first two for selling out their "principles". Very few people actually pay much attention to political developments at the local level as everyone's attention is focused on Moscow. Whereas in Moscow the main debate is on the pace of change, here the debate tends to center on who gets to reap the profits from change. Thus the organs of power are engaged in endless bickering over who has the right to parcel-out former State assets to the highest bidder.

St. Petersburg is run by a dual power structure. On one side sits the Mayor's office, the city's executive body, led by Anatoly Sobchak, and on the other side sits the City Council (or Council of People's Deputies as it is quaintly called), the city's legislative body. Until semi-democratic elections in 1989, the City Council was a rubber-stamp organ for the Communist Party leadership, though now they are feeling their oats and asserting themselves more forcefully in the decision-making process.

If you are lucky you may get to see a **political protest**. These usually take place in front of the City Council building if there is a session going on where some hot issue (the increase of transport tariffs, the mysterious disappearance of State funds designated for pensions, etc.) is being discussed. Otherwise the place of choice for demonstrations is by the Alexander Column in Palace Square. The most interesting protesters are the nationalists and neo-Bolsheviks who flock here every so often, waving placards of Stalin and Lenin around and blaming all of Russia's woes on an evil conspiracy between Zionists, imperialists, fascists and Boris Yeltsin. Be careful taking pictures at the more inflamed rallies; these people are very sensitive to these kinds of things and may express this sensitivity by punching you in the mouth. Nonetheless, most Russians look on politics with sheer apathy, a fact which is usually attributed to "the tremendous patience and endurance of the Russian people" which has let them get screwed by their leaders for countless centuries. Frustration is rampant and the lively ideological debates of the recent past seem irrelevant given most people's daily struggle to survive.

The Economic Situation

Russia is currently going through a very turbulent economic period and, barring several zillion dollars in foreign aid and investment, it is going to take some time for the economy to stand on its feet. The former centrally-planned and administered State sector is simultaneously being dismantled and collapsing of its own accord, resulting in serious dislocation and hardship for millions of people. In the old days, though things weren't great, everyone was able to get by with a bit of grit and hustle (though to hear some people tell it, the days of Brezhnev were the days of milk and honey and, more importantly, cheap plentiful vodka). Today the State is financially unable to support the citizens that kept it propped up for so long. State salaries (for doctors, teachers, government functionaries, etc.) are appallingly low, as are pensions, and child support is virtually non-existent.

On the other hand, St. Petersburg is teeming with a free-market frenzy that would give Adam Smith goosebumps. There has never been such a large selection of consumer goods available and all the wonderful manifestations of a new-born market economy (bribery, gambling, widespread prostitution and organized crime) are everywhere. The days of Five-Year Plans, fat subsidies and guaranteed employment are history.

As a foreigner with convertible currency, you are widely considered to be rich beyond means which is therefore license for anyone to try to squeeze as much out of you as possible on the scientifically proven theory that "$20 means a lot more to me than it does to you". Equally absurd are the incredible bargains to be found everywhere - 50 cent haircuts, $1 cab rides and so on. Try to be understanding of St. Petersburg's economic complexities and the position of its citizens, though not too understanding or you will be mercilessly taken to the cleaners.

Corollary #1: Inviting People to your Country
Very few Russians have been further west than Minsk and thus they are extremely fascinated by whatever's out there. Most people express a desire to go West for a look-round or, even better, to find some work and make some precious hard currency. We at Fresh Air certainly do. Most countries require that Russian citizens be officially invited by a native of that country before they can be eligible for a visa. Be aware that you will be responsible for the health, well-being and lawful conduct of your Russian guest(s). Should your guest be hospitalized or commit a major felony, you may be held responsible to pay their hospital bills or to serve some of their jail sentence for their actions in your country whilst on your invitation. Be careful and be sure. While we don't suggest that you categorically refuse to invite anyone, it couldn't hurt to check with your consulate or embassy as to both the procedures and the responsibilities.

Corollary #2: Love
"Russian woman, 24, will marry foreigner...". Ads like this appear in English-language newspapers here as well as in the twinkling eyes of attractive young women in microscopic skirts who hang out in hard currency bars. We wouldn't dare suggest that you're not the sexy hunk he or she says you are, but a foreign romantic partner is something very highly prized here, for both financial reasons and the exit potential. People

susceptible to heartbreak are advised to give some time to any romantic liason(s) entered into before making a commitment. If you are set on getting married, check with your consulate for immigration and naturalization procedures (we're sure your future spouse will also be interested in these procedures).

Corollary #3: Shady Business Deals
It is not uncommon for acquaintances to propose some kind of sweet sounding deal or joint venture. Though this may be the largest, richest and fastest growing market on the planet, common sense is still the most valuable local commodity. If it sounds too good to be true, it probably is. You may be a respected expert in your field back home, but the fact of the matter is you probably don't know *diddly-squat* about business realities here. It is worth mentioning that business trust is a two-sided coin and Russian business people are usually wary and slow to trust foreigners, very often with good reason. And if someone offers to sell you St. Isaac's Cathedral, don't believe it - we already traded it for the Golden Gate Bridge (and we got burned).

THE POPULACE

Russians are and have always been very warm, friendly people and they are generous and thoughtful hosts. Hands-on exposure to Western culture is still a relatively new thing here, and many people are endlessly fascinated by things we consider *passé*. It is common for people to invite you to their home, where you may be wined and dined and married off to the youngest sibling.

Keep in mind that like anywhere else St. Petersburg has its share of unsavory characters. You will undoubtedly notice (especially in bars, casinos, street corners and hip ruble restaurants) large, scarred men in leather jackets with crew cuts, crooked noses, no necks and calloused hands the size of basketballs. These are **goons** and should be left alone. The goon's car of choice is a muddy Mercedes Benz with no license plates or a black Lada four-door hatchback.

Note that Russia is an ethnic melting pot, and pride in one's ethnic identity is a growing trend as the bloody civil wars in the southern republics illustrate. The bankruptcy of Marxist-Leninist international consciousness and the current economic hardships have likewise led to an awakening of national consciousness amongst Russians. This Russian national awakening manifests itself in an acute interest in versions of Russian history and culture stripped of Communist ideological padding, as well as in a lot of finger-pointing in the direction of other nationalities as a way of explaining past and present problems. To use the term "Soviet" when you mean "Russian" is like asking a Canadian which state they're from, although there are plenty of things in this country which cannot be described in any way other than Soviet. Anyway, racial relations can be rather tense in this part of the world, so try your best to be sensitive to Russians, Buryats, Tadjiks, Kalmyks and the other 140 nationalities alike.

Practices and Customs
Russians are tremendous **gift givers** and the transfer of small tokens of generosity is quite an ingrained tradition. Friends and acquaintances love to present gifts to each other and this can be a great way to break the ice. The best gifts are of course things that are not readily available here and thus have some novelty value: kitschy postcards of your home country, replicas (little Statues of Liberty, Big Bens, etc.), coffee mugs with silly inscriptions and so on. Perfume samples, cosmetics, children's toys or clothes (Russians always bring something for kids), picture books, rock or pop music tapes, and any type of clothing will also be greatly appreciated.

Gifts are also given in order to grease wheels - whether it is in order to get a seat in a Russian restaurant that is ostensibly "booked solid", a train ticket, or an office on Nevsky Prospekt. This type of gift is also known as a **bribe** and is a part of day to day existence. Seventy-four years of Communism did to the working populace's motivation what neutering does to a cat's sex life - it's as if their incentive to do anything but make your life difficult was surgically removed. These little tokens serve to open all kinds of otherwise shut doors. The appropriate bribe depends on what you are trying to accomplish. A dollar or a bottle of something should conquer a doorman; on the other hand anyone wishing to rent the Hermitage for a private party may need to give a little more. Note that the influx of consumer goods has outdated many of the old cliché bribes. For instance, whereas in the old days a pack of Marlboro would stop traffic and a carton would get you a fat public works contract, nowadays they are available on every street corner and their bribe value has greatly diminished.

Tipping was abolished after the Revolution and it will take some time for the populace to get back into the habit again. This process is not particularly facilitated by the usually appalling levels of service here, though it's hard to say which is the cause and which is the effect. When you're in a Western establishment (a hotel or hard currency restaurant, for instance) you should tip as you do at home - the doorman, the cloakroom attendant, the waiter, the bartender, the cat, etc. With ruble establishments you should as a general rule leave a little something if the level of service merits it. Also tour guides, drivers and other people who spend more than a little time with you should be tipped or presented with something.

Smoking would appear to be almost mandatory and Western visitors will most likely be aghast at Russians' tolerant attitude towards it. Restaurants and cafes seem to feature two sections:

Smoking and Chain-Smoking. Russian cigarettes are particularly foul smelling and the cheaper the brand the more pungent the aroma. The most popular revolting smelling brands you'll encounter here are *Stewardess*, *Kosmos* and the thoroughly repulsive, unfiltered *Belomorkanal*. Asking someone near you to put out a cigarette is unlikely to be met with acquiescence. Smoking is not permitted, however, on public transport, although there are a variety of other scents, particularly during the summer, which produce more or less the same effect.

Although **sexism** in all its manifestations is being stamped out in the egalitarian West, its vestiges are still quite ingrained in this culture. It is considered proper for men to do things for women such as hold open doors for them, pour their drinks and serve their food first, assist them in and out of cars and buses, light their cigarettes for them (even if it means rubbing two sticks together) and help them put on and take off their coats. Likewise, there exists a pretty firm conception of the difference between "women's work" (everything) and "men's work" (hammering a couple of nails here and there in between bottles of vodka). Most Russians understand that we have different customs and attitudes, and won't be offended if we don't do the above things.

Some Local Habits

- It is considered disrespectful to shake hands while wearing gloves.

- When taking out a cigarette for yourself, always be sure to offer one to those around you.

- Never cross your legs in the American style (ankle resting on knee) as this is considered rude, especially if the sole of your shoe or foot is visible.

- Russians tend to be excellent housekeepers, so when entering a Russian household, always stop inside the entranceway and remove your shoes. You will be given slippers (*tapochki*) to wear while inside.

- When invited to someone's home, bring a gift - the standard is a bottle of something, flowers or something sweet to have with tea.

- Wait fifteen minutes before getting angry when someone is late, at least a half hour before storming off in a huff, or ninety minutes before leaving in an hour and a huff.

- Things are bad enough here so don't rub it in by complaining or always comparing things to your country.

In Russia it is polite to address a person either by their last name (e.g. "Mr. Lenin") or, more commonly, by their name and patronymic, a derivative of their father's name (e.g. "Vladimir Ilyich"). This is especially the case for elders, for instance someone's *babushka*, and with important politicos and businessmen.

Russians are, generally speaking, rather **superstitious**. It is unlikely that people will perform strange rituals if you break one, but we'll list a few superstitions in the hope that awkward situations can thus be avoided. It is considered bad luck to shake hands or kiss through a doorway. If you step on someone's foot, you should let them step on yours in return (hopefully the person is not wearing cleats). Giving someone an even number of flowers will bring them bad luck. And, if you are standing in between two people who have the same first name (which happens quite frequently as 70% of the population is named Natasha or Sasha), make a wish and spin around on your left leg three times for the wish to come true.

Holidays

Jan 7* - Russian Orthodox Christmas, the most important Church holiday of the year.

Feb 23 - Soviet Army Day. Although this is not a public holiday, and the Soviet Army does not exist any more, this day is considered a sort of "Men's Day" as all young men are required to serve in the military.

March 8 - International Women's Day. On this day it is important to at least phone all your female acquaintances and wish them well, and to give gifts to those you are closer to.

March/April - Russian Orthodox Easter, the second most important Church holiday.

May 1 - International Workers' Solidarity Day (three day weekend of drinking).

May 9 - Victory Day (three day weekend, more drinking).

May 27- St. Petersburg's birthday (drink toasts to the city).

June 12 - Independence Day (drink toasts to independence).

Dec 31-Jan 1 - New Year (two weeks of drinking).

---

*Note that until February 14, 1918, Russia used the Julian calendar, which was thirteen days behind the Gregorian calendar in use across Europe. Because of this, Christmas is in January, the October Revolution was celebrated in November, and many people celebrate New Year's Eve twice - on December 31 and on January 13 (and every night in between).

WHAT TO BRING

A couple of years ago anyone coming to St. Petersburg pretty much had to pack everything with them as there were few things not in the tuber family available in the stores. Things have changed so rapidly that now almost everything you may need is available, though generally the more specific the item, the more searching it will take to find it.

Health insurance is never a bad idea for any traveller, especially in a country like Russia where the health care tends to leave much to be desired. If you're coming in the summer months, some **mosquito repellant** is a must; remember, Petersburg was built on a swamp. People planning on renting an apartment and staying for a while should bring **spices** with them and any other specific cooking items that may be desired, and a **water purification** filter or tablets will also come in handy. Students who are here for three months or longer must present the educational institution with an **AIDS test** proving they are HIV-negative, or else they will test you here and you don't want them to do that. Speaking of which, it is good to bring some sterile **needles and syringes** with you in case of a medical emergency, as well as any **prescription medicines** you may need. **English-language books** are in short supply here and the selection is heavy on the pulp so readers are advised to pack their own. During the rainy and snowy months the city can get quite gushy so some **galoshes** or good **boots** will keep the feets happy. Many of the standard cliché items (sanitary napkins, toilet paper) are pretty readily available in both hard currency and ruble stores, so you won't need a year's supply, but definitely **bring a towel** as Russian towels are usually the size of this book and less absorbent as well.

AND NOW A DISCLAIMER

One thing that should serve to confuse visitors to St. Petersburg is that the names of many streets and locations are being changed. Old standardized Soviet names (Third Five-Year Plan Avenue, Communist International Square, Boulevard of Some Eastern European Puppet Leader) are being replaced with their pre-Revolutionary names, and it is going to take some time for locals to get used to this as well as for street signs and metro recordings to change. We have listed all the new names according to the most recent name-changing decree, but there is no question that more will come, and apparently some anti-Soviet enthusiasts are putting up signs with the pre-Revolutionary names themselves. **Appendix 1** is a list of all the officially changed names. Be aware that the recording that announces metro stations may not have been changed, although the signs have; in order to avoid confusion you should learn both old and new names.

HISTORY

S T. PETERSBURG IS INEXORABLY linked with the personality of its founder, Tsar **Peter I**. Peter was the grandson of Mikhail Romanov, founder of the Romanov dynasty which ruled Russia from 1613 until 1917. The son of Tsar Alexis (1645-1676) from his second marriage, Peter rose to power despite meddling by jealous relatives from Alexis' first marriage. The most menacing of these was Sophie, Alexis' daughter and the older sister of Peter's physically and mentally retarded half-brother Ivan. Ivan and Peter, both kids, were declared co-tsars in 1681 and then sent off to play while Sophie ruled as Regent. Whereas Ivan remained unfit for duty as a ruler for his entire short life, Peter learned military skills and built up loyalty in the most influential regiments during his half-sister's regency. In 1689 Peter returned to Moscow, deposed her and shipped her off to a convent.

Peter inherited a Russia that was too backward for his taste. Trade was relatively undeveloped due to the lack of access to a warm-water port (the Baltic belonged to the Swedes and the Black Sea was in Turkish hands) and the populace, even the aristocracy, was for the most part uneducated. Peter was determined to modernize Russia regardless of the cost, and immediately after Ivan's death in 1696 left him as sole sovereign he took off on a two year fact-finding and recruitment mission across Europe.

Peter's first goal was to turn Russia into a formidable naval power. He had seen navies and wanted one too. With this in mind he attacked both north and south, taking the Azov Sea from the Turks in the south in 1696 and then in 1703 driving the Swedes from the Neva delta, seizing the fortress-town Noteburg and renaming it Schlüsselburg (now called Petrokrepost). In order to strengthen the northern position

Peter decided to build a second fortress on the Neva delta that would eventually become his new capital.

He Built it on a Swamp

On May 16, 1703, Peter laid the first stone of the fortress he named St. Petersburg in honor of St. Peter, guardian of the gates of Heaven. Across the river from the fortress Peter built a shipyard (the Admiralty). Peter then figured why not build a city around his little fortress and shipyard, providing Russia with a trading port and a "window onto Europe" through which Russia could hopefully catch Poland in her underwear.

Geological conditions presented Peter with a formidable challenge. In many areas the ground was so soft that huge wooden planks had to be laid as foundations to prevent buildings from sinking. During the initial phases of construction thousands of peasants and workers died of malaria or scurvy and many were picked off by marauding wolves, earning Petersburg the epithet "the city laid on bones". In 1712 Peter decided to make St. Petersburg Russia's capital and required the aristocratic families to move here and build lavish homes for themselves (at their own expense), as well as chip in to help build government buildings.

Petersburg after Peter

The 18th century saw Petersburg develop not only into Russia's political and economic center but into its cultural center as well. Russian and European culture met in St. Petersburg, with more and more members of the aristocracy studying abroad and learning foreign languages at home. While the rest of Russia remained mired in backwardness, Petersburg flourished under the auspices of the nobility and the merchant classes that were based here. By the end of the 18th century secular literature and art (previously forbidden) had begun to develop, setting the stage for the tremendous flowering of the arts during the 19th century.

A Few Intrigues
For the 71 years after Peter the Great's death Russia was almost exclusively ruled by women. The first four decades saw a series of empresses who, once they stepped over their rivals to get to the throne, administered Russia with little innovation. Peter's second wife, **Catherine I,** ruled briefly until 1727, followed by Peter the Great's grandson **Peter II** who died of smallpox in 1730 at the age of 17. The throne then passed to **Anna**, daughter of Peter the Great's half-brother Ivan. She ruled until 1740, nominating her older sister's grandson, the two-month old **Ivan VI**, to succeed her. At first the Empress Anna's favorite, Ernst Büren, was named Regent but he was deposed within three weeks and Ivan VI's mother (who was also called Anna) was given the regency. After a year the Grand Duchess **Elizabeth**, Peter the Great's last surviving child, seized power and had the one year old Ivan VI locked up in the Schlüsselburg Fortress with instructions to kill him if he tried to escape. So it is safe to conclude that Ivan VI had a pretty miserable childhood.*

Lesson One: Be Nice to Your Wife
Elizabeth had no children and ended up leaving the throne to her nephew, Charles Peter Ulrich of Holstein (**Peter III**). Peter assumed the throne in January 1762 and within six months he had managed to alienate everyone with his Prussophilia, offenses against the Orthodox Church and his boyish obsession with guns and the military. His wife, the German born Sophie of Anhalt-Zerbst, took to Russia much better than Peter did, learning the language and adopting Orthodoxy. Sophie (rechristened Catherine) had Peter III arrested in June 1762 and she forced him to abdicate in her favor. One week later he died in somewhat mysterious circumstances.

---

*Ivan wasn't given much of a chance to make something of his adulthood; he was killed in 1764 during a failed rescue attempt.

Catherine the Great
Of all the empresses, Catherine II (later known as **Catherine the Great**) deserves special note. She combined an avid personal interest in Enlightenment ideas (she was quite well-read and corresponded with Diderot, Voltaire and d'Alembert) with the unbending conviction that autocracy was the only thing that could handle Russia. Under her rule Russia experienced a "golden age of the nobility" where the aristocracy was permitted to forego State service and concentrate on their own personal affairs. The Russian Empire expanded into the Crimea and, together with Prussia and Austria, partitioned Poland three times, controlling Warsaw until 1918. Under Catherine, Russia grew into the great European power Peter the Great had envisioned one hundred years before. And though it is common knowledge that she had quite a voracious sexual appetite, the legend about the horse is just not true.

Lesson Two: Be Nice to Your Son
Catherine's son, **Paul I,** assumed the throne in 1796. Like Peter III, Paul exhibited a manic love of all things military, drilling his troops incessantly and even becoming Grand Poobah of the Knights of Malta. His unpredictability and paranoia made him both feared and hated by the court, and in 1801 he was deposed by guard officers and disaffected courtiers with the tacit agreement of his eldest son, Alexander. During the coup Paul was accidently murdered by the intoxicated conspirators.

How One Little Frenchman Can Ruin Your Day
Having observed the political lessons of the 18th century (notably the French Revolution and its rather unhealthy consequence for a particular monarch), Alexander recognized the need to overhaul his country somehow. He was distracted however by Napoleon who in 1812 sent an army of 600,000 in Alexander's general direction, eventually taking Moscow. That winter the Russians turned the tide against the pesky little

Corsican, destroying most of the invading army and marching victoriously into Paris. After the victory Alexander went weird, becoming so wrapped up in what he saw as his divine mission to preserve autocracy on the planet that reforms became of little concern to him and nothing major was accomplished. Still, the economic and social problems Russia faced did not disappear, and many of the officers who saw Europe during the war grew increasingly resentful at their lack of say in how things were run in Russia.

The Decembrists' Revolt
Anti-authoritarian sentiments burst into open demonstration when Alexander died in December of 1825. The throne passed to his younger brother **Nicholas I**, who had a reputation as an autocratic hard-ass. A group of disgruntled army officers gathered in Senate Square, proclaimed their loyalty to Nicholas' older brother Constantine and demanded such outrageous things as representation in the government and an end to serfdom. Nicholas responded by bringing in loyal troops and forcing the rebels (later known as Decembrists) to surrender. They were sent to the dungeons at the Peter and Paul Fortress and that was the last Russia heard of reform for a while.

There is no question that this revolt, combined with the waning of autocracy across Europe, profoundly affected Nicholas I's way of thinking. Fearing revolution in any shape or form, his reign became intensely repressive, with censorship heavily enforced, education abroad curtailed and a system of secret police and internal spies put into operation. Nonetheless Petersburg was buzzing with underground discussion groups working out alternative ideas and philosophies, and Russia experienced a golden age of literature with Pushkin, Lermontov and Gogol writing their seminal works and Dostoevsky and Turgenev launching their literary careers.

Serf's Up

When **Alexander II** assumed the throne in 1855 Russia had more problems than an epileptic tight-rope walker. Nicholas' imperialist pretensions towards Turkey left Russia embroiled in the embarrassing Crimean War with France and Britain, and discontent both among the upper classes and the serfs was becoming more evident (during Nicholas' reign there had been over 500 peasant uprisings). A series of reforms including the abolition of flogging in the army and some judicial and educational reforms culminated in the abolition of serfdom in 1861. After an assassination attempt on Alexander II in 1866, the reform period gradually faded and Russia slid back into conservatism.

During the 1860s and 1870s revolutionary groups began to flower in St. Petersburg, mostly among students. The 1860s were the heydey of the nihilists, 19th century hippies who offended people with their hair styles and free-loving attitudes. In the 1870s populism was the rage and young starry-eyed revolutionaries "went to the people" (i.e. travelled to peasant communes in an attempt to put their theories about the political potential of the Russian countryside into practice) only to have the people tell them to get lost. Anarchists and terrorists also appeared, and it was one of the latter (representing an extremist group called People's Will) that assassinated Alexander II on March 1, 1881.

No More Mr. Nice Guy

The last two tsars rejected the idea that the autocracy needed reforming from above and the gap between the authorities and the people continued to widen. Tsar **Alexander III** hunted out terrorists and revolutionaries, tightened censorship and reined in the educational and judicial systems. It was also at this time that Russia embarked down the path of industrialization with massive factories appearing in the Petersburg area. Working conditions were miserable and social tension continued to grow as more and more people came to believe that only revolution could bring about social, economic and political change.

The last Tsar, **Nicholas II**, was not so much a bad man as just a Clark Kent when Russia needed a Superman, or at least an Aquaman. His wife Alexandra totally dominated him, and together they were unprepared to deal with the tremendous crises that faced Russia. His reign was punctuated with one disaster after another, from worker and peasant uprisings to defeat in war with Japan, and his final rating as tsar suffered a lot from the fact that the 400 year Romanov Dynasty ended during his reign.

The First Russian Revolution
The first major disaster happened on January 9, 1905. A crowd of workers led by the Orthodox priest Father Gapon marched to Palace Square with a peaceful petition asking for better working conditions. Troops opened fire on the marchers and in the ensuing panic about one hundred died and thousands were wounded in what came to be known as "Bloody Sunday". As a result there were mutinies, murders of landowners and industrialists, strikes and enough general hubbub to force Nicholas to make some concessions in order to avert total disaster. The Tsar issued the so-called "October Manifesto" which established a constitutional body (called the Duma) and promised civil rights and liberties to all, though Nicholas eventually went back on most of these promises and political tension continued to build until 1914 when an external threat gave him a temporary reprieve.

World War and Revolution
At the onset of World War I Russians heeded the call for unity in order to concentrate on the war effort and, in a show of anti-German feeling, St. Petersburg was given the more Russian sounding name of Petrograd. However, after a couple of years of drawn-out, inconclusive fighting the masses started getting restless once again. The government was essentially para-

lyzed as Nicholas had gone off to the front to oversee the war effort and his assertive wife had fallen under the influence of the funky monk Rasputin who packed government positions with corrupt and ineffectual friends. Eventually, in February of 1917, food riots brought angry crowds to Palace Square and this time policemen and soldiers refused to fire on them. A Provisional Government was declared and Tsar Nicholas was forced to abdicate.

The Provisional Government was essentially crippled from its birth by divisions on a number of issues, particularly on whether Russia should continue the war effort and on the scope and scale of the revolutionary changes. The Provisional Government was to serve until elections could be held in November for a national Constituent Assembly which would use its mandate to lead the country out of chaos. The Germans, wanting Russian out of the war, provided Lenin with transport back home where he immediately started agitating for the Bolsheviks to seize power and declare peace.

As 1917 progressed the situation in Petersburg and on the Front continued to worsen and the Bolsheviks' slogan of "Peace, Bread, Land and Workers' Control" resonated deeper and deeper. Lenin saw his opportunity and on the night of October 24 the Bolsheviks' Red Army garrisons quietly seized government buildings and communication centers, arresting members of the Provisional Government and declaring a new government of the Soviets (as the Councils of Workers' and Soldiers' Deputies were called). This *coup d'état* came to be known as the **October Revolution**.

A Capital Shake-up
Elections to the Constituent Assembly were held as scheduled, but when the results did not suit the Bolsheviks (they received only 15% of the vote whereas their rivals, the rural-based Socialist Revolutionaries, received over 55%), the Red Army

dissolved the Assembly and arrested its members. What followed was three years of violent bloodshed as Russia withdrew from World War I and fell into Civil War. Despite fierce resistance across the countryside, the Bolsheviks prevailed and by the end of 1920 the country had for the most part been pacified. Victims of the Civil War and the subsequent Red Terror proclaimed by Lenin to suppress counter-revolution and consolidate power numbered in the millions.

Fearing foreign intervention and wanting to make a break from the Tsarist past, the Bolsheviks moved the capital from St. Petersburg to Moscow in 1918. A depleted Petersburg took a back seat as Moscow re-emerged as Russia's political and economic center. The privations of the World War, Revolution and Civil War drove many of Petersburg's inhabitants out to the countryside, and by 1920 less than one third of Petersburg's 1916 population remained in the city.

Stalin, who emerged victorious from the power struggle following Lenin's death in 1924, despised Petersburg and its ties with both Tsarism and the Old Revolutionaries who overthrew it. Throughout his career as Party Leader he viewed Leningrad (as they renamed Petrograd after Lenin's death) as a threat and a potential rival to his power. In 1934 the charismatic and popular Leningrad Party Leader Sergei Kirov was assassinated in his office, most likely by a secret agent under Stalin's orders. This marked the beginning of the **Great Purges** which lasted until 1938, during which millions of people were killed or sent to labor camps (*gulags*) on little or no foundation. Almost all of the Old Bolsheviks were arrested, tortured, publicly tried and summarily shot after confessing to absurd fabricated crimes. The labor camps' population in 1938 reached 8 million, and most inmates did not survive. As a result of this reign of terror a generation of bureaucrats rose that was absolutely loyal to Stalin.

The Great Patriotic War
What the rest of the planet calls World War II is known here as
the **Great Patriotic War** and is dated from 1941 until 1945 (the
years of the Molotov-Ribbentrop Non-Aggression Pact are
conveniently left out). Within 4 months of Hitler's invasion on
June 22, 1941, Nazi troops had taken Kiev and were on the
outskirts of both Moscow and Leningrad. Hitler ordered his
troops to wipe Leningrad off the face of the earth and they
blockaded the city for 900 days, shelling incessantly in an
attempt to destroy the population's will. Leningrad did not
give in and the blockade was eventually broken on January 27,
1944, but only after well over half a million civilians had
perished.

Post-war Letdown
The naive hope that Stalin would reward the victorious Soviet
Union by easing up on his heavy-handed policies proved to be
misguided. The Orthodox Church, which enjoyed a few years
of relative rehabilitation in order to help foster wartime unity,
was again repressed, and many repatriated citizens were sent
to *gulags* as politically suspect together with some of the
soldiers who fought in Europe. Stalin particularly hated the
solidarity that the blockade experience had created amongst
Leningraders and ruthlessly purged the city's Party leadership in the late 1940s.

Leningrad started rebuilding itself immediately after the War,
a Herculean task considering that one third of the city's
buildings had been damaged and much of its infrastructure
(factories, power stations, transportation networks, etc.) de-
stroyed. Following Stalin's death things here stayed reasonably calm through the **Khrushchev** and **Brezhnev** years.
Moscow was the undisputed center of the USSR although
Leningrad remained Russia's cultural center, with many excit-
ing innovations in art, popular music and literature originat-
ing here.

Democracy in Petersburg

In the local elections of March, 1989, Leningraders were given a choice of Communist Party members to vote for and they elected their first quasi-democratic City Council. One of these new Deputies was a little-known lawyer by the name of **Anatoly Sobchak** who squeaked by after two run-offs to win his district. Sobchak rose to the helm of a group of reform-minded Deputies and in 1990 was elected Petersburg's Mayor. Under his leadership the city has slowly opened itself to foreign investment and free-market development. Leningraders overwhelmingly voted in 1991 to rename their city St. Petersburg and, with the opening of Russia, the historic capital has once again come to life as a meeting place of East and West.

COMING AND GOING

THOUGH NOT AS DIFFICULT as getting into the USSR was, getting into Russia can still present a logistical challenge to the prospective visitor. Visas are required for citizens of all Western countries. The cost, difficulty and time necessary to obtain a visa varies depending on the visitor's nationality, the country where the visa is being issued and the current work-load of that particular visa department. As with all formalities concerning Russia and the former Soviet Republics, visa procedures are in a constant, almost fluid state of change so checking with your nearest Russian Embassy or Consulate for the *visa regulation of the week* is an advisable first step to planning any visit to Russia.

Types of Visas and How to Get Them
There are four types of visas: Tourist, Commercial, Student and Private. In order to receive any visa you must present a Russian Consular Office with a voucher from a tourist agency or a confirmed hotel reservation, a written invitation from a Russian business, proof of enrollment in an educational program, or an official invitation from a Russian citizen. In addition, you must provide three passport-size photos, a visa application statement (available from the Consular Office), your passport (in some countries a photocopy of your passport will suffice) and a fee in local currency. The Consulate will advise you on costs and time required to issue your visa although in all Consulates a special "rush fee" will speed up the process considerably and may even produce a same day visa, but don't count on it. We recommend that despite any signs of disorganization and absurdity (common phenomena in Russian Consular Offices), you remain polite and friendly lest a consular officer takes a dislike to you and arbitrarily delays issuing your visa until 1998. Look upon any inconveniences you may have in getting your visa as training for your trip to Russia.

The person or organization who provides you with the necessary documentation to obtain your visa (i.e. your tour operator, local business or citizen) takes responsibility for your actions while you are in the country. Should you violate the law or the terms of your visa, both you and this individual or organization will be held liable for any resulting fines.

To receive a **tourist visa** you will need to present the Consular Office with proof that you have a confirmed hotel reservation in your destination city. Most hotels can provide this by fax (see *Accommodation*) and some hotels have international booking agents that can do this outside of Russia. Hotels usually require pre-payment of some sort, so don't count on using a random hotel as a vehicle for getting a visa. Budget travellers can make reservations at and get visa support from the St. Petersburg Youth Hostel (see *Accommodation*). An alternative is to use a tourist agency to arrange your visa to Russia. Vouchers from accredited organizations serve the same purpose as confirmed hotel reservations.

A **commercial visa** is issued to supposed colleagues of a local firm that has clearance from the Ministry of Foreign Affairs to issue work invitations. These invitations must be on company letterhead, signed and stamped with the ubiquitous, big round Russian stamp. Along with the usual personal information (passport number, date of its expiry, date of birth and sex), the invitation should state the purpose of your visit (for example, "to take part in negotiations"). The inviting company must also petition the Ministry to send a telex to the issuing Consular Office giving you *visa support*, without which you are unlikely to receive anything but dirty looks.

A **student visa** can only be issued by accredited educational institutions that accept foreigners (for a list of language schools see *Language*). They usually require a good deal of advance preparation and programs are not cheap. On the other hand, having a student visa entitles you to occasional discounts on

plane and train transportation and visa fees for some former republics.

People with friends, relatives or other connections who are Russian citizens can be issued a **private visa** upon presentation of an *izveshcheniye* (извещение). To get this, the Russian host must fill out an invitation form at their local Department of Visas and Registration (OVIR) office. After a time, usually a few weeks, they will receive the извещение form which they must somehow get to you. This form is then presented to your Russian Consular Office, together with the other requisites, and processed into a visa.

Standard visas are one-time (однократная) entry-exit. Visas can be extended in OVIR upon presentation of a petition from the organization or person that invited you, though tourist visas are rarely extended for more than a few days. Do not wait until the last minute to extend your visa, because if something goes wrong (as it inevitably will) you could face problems when the original visa expires.

OVIR Offices in St. Petersburg

Central office: *Ulitsa Saltykova-Shchedrina 4. Metro: Chernyshevskaya. Tel: 278 2481.*

Dzerzhinsky region: *Ulitsa Chekhova 15. Metro: Chernyshevskaya. Tel: 272 5556.*

Frunzensky region: *Naberezhnaya Obvodnogo Kanala 48. Metro: Frunzenskaya. Tel: 166 1468.*

Kalininsky region: *Mineralnaya Ulitsa 3. Metro: Ploshchad Lenina. Tel: 540 3987.*

Kirovsky region: *Prospekt Stachek 18. Metro: Narvskaya. Tel: 252 7714.*

Krasnoselsky region: *Avangardnaya Ulitsa 35. Metro: Prospekt Veteranov then trolley 20, 32 or 37. Tel: 136 8906.*

Kuibyshevsky region: *Pereulok Krylova 3. Metro: Gostiny Dvor. Tel: 310 4117.*

Leninsky region: *Sovietsky Pereulok 9. Metro: Tekhnologichesky Institut. Tel: 292 4356.*

Moskovsky region: *Moskovsky Prospekt 95. Metro: Moskovskaya Vorota. Tel: 298 1827.*

Nevsky region: *Ulitsa Zubkovskaya 4. Metro: Elizarovskaya. Tel: 560 9969.*

Novocherkassky region: *Krasnodonskaya Ulitsa 14.   Metro: Novocherkasskaya then tram 23 or 46. Tel: 224 0196.*

Oktyabrsky region: *Bolshaya Podyacheskaya Ulitsa 26. Metro: Sadovaya/ Sennaya Ploshchad. Tel: 314 4901.*

Petrogradsky region: *Bolshaya Monetnaya Ulitsa 20. Metro: Gorkovskaya. Tel: 232 1119.*

Primorsky region: *Ulitsa Generala Khruleva 15. Metro: Pionerskaya. Tel: 394 7213.*

Smolninsky region: *Mytninskaya Ulitsa 3. Metro: Ploshchad Vosstaniya. Tel: 274 5710.*

Vasileostrovsky region: *19th Liniya 10. Metro: Vasileostrovskaya. Tel: 355 7524.*

Vyborgsky region: *Lesnoi Prospekt 20. Metro: Vyborgskaya. Tel: 542 2172.*

OVIR is open for foreigners on Mondays and Wednesdays from 10:00-12:00 and Fridays from 14:00-16:00.

Registration

You are required to **register your visa** within 24 hours of arrival in the country (if you arrive on a weekend or holiday, register the first available day). For tourist visas it is assumed that the tourist agency or hotel that issued the invitation will take care of this; if they don't, you could be in for a nasty surprise if it gets noticed on your way out of the country. Commercial visas are registered in the local OVIR office by a letter from the inviting company. Private visas are registered by the person who issued the invitation. Since it is theoretically illegal to spend unregistered time in this country, it's best to just register so they have one less reason to hassle you when you leave.

Your visa is an important document. It will be checked upon arrival, in customs and when leaving the country. Safeguard it. Citizens from Western countries do not receive stamps in their passports, but rather stamps on their visas which are taken back from you when you leave. Upon checking into your hotel, you will be required to give them your passport and visa for OVIR registration. You will be able to retrieve them after a day or so, but as you will probably not need them while in the city (except when buying rail or airline tickets and when changing travellers cheques), it's a good idea to leave them with the hotel. You should bring photocopies of your passport and visa. Carrying these around is safe, adequate for most identification purposes and, if your documents are stolen, photocopies make replacing them infinitely easier.

Lost or stolen passports can be replaced at your country's consular office in St. Petersburg or, if your country does not have a consulate in town, at your embassy in Moscow. To replace a lost or stolen passport you will need proof of citizenship and, if the passport was stolen, a police report stating the circumstances of the theft.

CUSTOMS

Customs laws change more frequently than any other type of laws here (with the laws on hard currency operations running a close second), and the only things that remain consistent are that they are hard to find out, confusing and subject to spontaneous modification at the customs official's whim.

Arrival
As you arrive into Russia you will need to fill out a **Customs and Currency Declaration Statement** which must list all foreign currency (including travellers cheques) you are bringing into the country. Be sure to also put down as much identifying information as possible about any items of value you have so that when you leave you don't have to pay outrageous customs tariffs on your own stuff. Include watches, cameras, jewelry, explosives, etc. The customs official will scribble something on the form, stamp it and give it back to you. Do not lose it unless the prospect of being at the total mercy of a sadistic official when you are leaving excites you in any way.

Departure
Customs officials are experts at sniffing out large stashes of caviar, amber, expensive artwork and uranium so shoppers of all kinds should keep receipts of anything bought in case they decide to enforce the law on you five minutes before your plane takes off. Anything that vaguely resembles **art** should be cleared in advance through the local representative of the Ministry of Culture located at *Kanal Griboyedova 107* (*Metro: Sadovaya and walk down the canal towards the Mariinsky Theater*). Bring the receipt and the item, though photographs of the item will do if it's too large to lug. There they will debate whether the item bears any "historical significance"; if so, you're bumming the hairpiece as it will not be allowed to leave the country. Otherwise they'll just assess its value and slap a tariff

on it. Most art galleries will clear works through customs for you, though getting a stamped receipt from the guy outside the Hermitage who sells you a Van Gogh is pretty unlikely. Failure to clear things in advance will result in significantly higher tariffs, bullying and possible confiscation by the customs official.

BY PLANE

Pulkovo II International Airport is located 17 kilometers south of the city. Flights arrive at and depart from Pulkovo on the State airline Aeroflot and many major international carriers. The domestic airport is **Pulkovo I**, located slightly further to the south along the same road as Pulkovo II. Almost all major cities of the former Soviet Union can be reached directly on Aeroflot, but flights to all but the most major hubs are irregular so you may need to go by way of Moscow.

Both Pulkovo I and II are "no-frills" airports; if you need help toting bags or getting from the airport into town, try to arrange this in advance as carts and rides are not always easy to locate. Adding to the confusion, Pulkovo II is undergoing renovation (they are scheduled to complete the arrival terminal in the summer of 1993, but they were also scheduled to have built Communism by 1961 so who really knows). There are some tourist services available including duty-free shops, snack bars and public telephones (which you won't be able to use because you won't have the necessary coins with you). Airline offices are in the main building on the second floor.

There are **taxis** waiting at the airport. Like airport taxis worldwide, they will try to extract as much money from you as possible, usually no less than $20 for a ride into the city, and would sooner swallow dynamite than accept rubles. If you are booked into a major hotel they can arrange to have you picked up.

There are also **public buses** for the truly intrepid: number 13 from Pulkovo II; 39 and 80 from Pulkovo I. Sometimes hours can go by without the appearance of one of these buses, much to the delight of the taxi drivers, and they are often so full that even a person without luggage has a hard time squeezing on. This option is only recommended for experienced Russia travellers or those wanting a crash immersion into some of the wonders of everyday Russian life. After a few stops (15 minutes) you will be at the Moskovskaya Metro station (blue line), one stop past the hard-to-miss Monument to the Heroic Defenders of Leningrad. Look for a large "M" and a stairway going down and quickly turn to the *Moving Around the City* section.

Airline Tickets and Reservations
With international airlines' growing interest in St. Petersburg, making reservations and purchasing airline tickets is easier than it used to be. Whenever possible, deal directly with the airline if they have a representative office here. Last minute arrangements can be difficult and making reservations well in advance is highly recommended, especially when dealing with Aeroflot. Many of the major hotel service bureaus can help make reservations and **American Express** operates a full service travel agency in the Grand Hotel Europe.

Austrian Airlines, **SAS**, and **Swissair** share a full service ticketing center at the entrance to the Nevskij Palace Arcade which makes things easy for incoming and outgoing fliers. Speedy ticketing is usually not a problem. There is also a ticketing office open every day at Pulkovo II International Airport. *Nevsky Prospekt 57. Metro: Mayakovskaya. Open 09:00-16:00 Mon-Fri. Major credit cards accepted. Tel: 314 5086, 311 6112; Fax: 164 7873. Pulkovo II tel: 104 3443.*

Other Airline Offices

Aeroflot (main booking office).   Useful if your last resort falls through. *Nevsky Prospekt 7/9. Metro: Nevsky Prospekt. Open 08:00-20:00 Mon-Fri. Tel: 314 6959.*

Air France *Pulkovo II. Open 09:00-18:00 Mon-Fri, 11:00-17:00 Sat, Sun. Tel: 104 3433.*

Balkan Airlines *Ulitsa Gertsena 36. Metro: Nevksy Prospekt. Open 09:00-17:00 (13:00-14:00) Mon-Fri. Tel: 315 5030.*

CSA Czech Airlines *Ulitsa Gertsena 38. Metro: Nevsky Prospekt. Open 09:00-17:00 (13:00-14:00) Mon-Fri. Tel: 315 5259.*

Delta Airlines *Ulitsa Gertsena 36. Metro: Nevksy Prospekt. Open 09:00-17:00 (13:00-14:00) Mon-Fri. Tel: 311 5819.*

Finnair *Ulitsa Gogolya 19. Metro: Nevsky Prospekt. Open 09:00-17:00 Mon-Fri, 09:00-13:00 Sat. Tel: 315 9736.*

KLM *Pulkovo II. Open 09:00-13:00 daily. Tel: 104 3440.*

LOT Polish Airlines *Ulitsa Karavannaya 1. Metro: Gostiny Dvor. Open 10:00-18:00 Mon-Fri. Tel: 272 2982.*

Lufthansa *Voznesensky Prospekt 7. Metro: Sadovaya. Open 10:00-17:00 Mon-Fri. Tel: 314 4979.*

Malev Airlines *Voznesensky Prospekt 7. Metro: Sadovaya. Open 09:00-17:00 Mon-Fri. Tel: 315 5455.*

BY TRAIN

Train Stations

St. Petersburg has five train stations, each conveniently located near a metro station and named after their primary destination. Unfortunately, the user-friendliness ends there. Long lines, a complicated scheduling and ticketing system and an almost complete lack of foreign-language support can intimidate the inexperienced. Surging crowds, pickpockets, bums, thugs and the fact that most foreigners stick out like sore thumbs make St. Petersburg's train stations unfavorable places to hang around any longer than necessary. Some of them are particularly seedy (Moskovsky, Varshavsky, Baltiisky) and can be downright dangerous at night. Taxis lurk around the exits of all the train stations and they will take you places for inflated prices, usually in hard currency, though not as much as the ridiculous sums extracted at the airport.

Long Distance Train Tickets and Reservations
Both domestic and international train tickets can be purchased at the **Central Railway Agency** at *Naberezhnaya Kanala Griboyedova 24*, next to Kazansky Cathedral just off Nevsky Prospekt (look for a vertical sign with a locomotive on it). Bring your **passport and visa**. For tickets to destinations in Russia and the former Soviet Union, go in the main entrance, turn immediately to the right, go right again and up the stairs to Hall 3, windows 100-103, marked "Kassa Intourist" (Касса Интуриста). Foreigners on tourist visas will have to pay hard currency for their tickets; those on private or commercial visas pay the normal ruble price plus a small surcharge. The lines here aren't too long and, in theory, the workers are trained to deal with language barriers better than regular cashiers (which isn't saying a lot). Note that only one ticket can be sold per passport, so if you are buying for other people remember to bring their passports along. Alternatively, for no lines and ultimate convenience, tickets can be bought from tourist hotels for hard currency.

Types of Tickets
First class tickets are called SV or *lyuks*, and are two-person compartments. Not too many trains offer these, though most trains to Moscow and international destinations do. Four-person sleepers are called *kupei*. *Platskart* is the next lower class, where about 12 people share a large, semi-open compartment. All of these classes come with seat reservations and in sleepers you will be charged a fee for linen. There are a couple of classes lower than this but if you're adventurous enough to

take them then you won't need us giving you smart-ass descriptions of them.

Take with you any food and drink you might want for the journey as there will most probably be nothing available on board the train, although each carriage has a *samovar* of boiling water for tea or coffee.

International rail tickets are sold for hard currency to Russians and foreigners alike. There are different windows for different destinations: Poland, Romania, Bulgaria and Czechoslovakia (or whatever they're calling it these days) on the ground floor, in Hall 1, windows 80, 81, 83, 87 and 88; Germany, Hungary and what's left of Yugoslavia on the second floor, Hall 2, windows 90 and 91; Finland and Scandinavia on the second floor, Hall 2, window 94.

Try to avoid last minute bookings if at all possible. Neither the hotels nor the Intourist Kassas have a large supply of same-day tickets. For spontaneous train travel you will need to go to the appropriate train station and line up at the same-day (суточная) kassa and attempt to make yourself understood.

Local Trains
The *elektrichka*, or local suburban trains, are...shall we say...historic? Tickets are absurdly cheap and can be bought at the appropriate stations at windows labelled "Пригородные кассы" or from automatic machines with complicated instructions in Russian. Not the most comfortable way to travel; wooden benches, often baking hot during the summer, bitterly cold in the winter and jam-packed on weekends (especially to Pushkin), and they can be creepy late at night. These trains do not spend much time at stops and the garbled voice that announces the stations is almost impossible to understand so know in advance which stop is yours (maps are posted in the train stations and in some of the wagons).

Train Stations

Moscow Station or *Moskovsky Vokzal* handles trains to and from Moscow, northern Russia, Central Asia, Georgia, the Caucasus and the Crimea. Be warned that this is one of the seediest places in town. There are several daily trains **to Moscow**, with the night trains being preferable; they take about eight hours and leave around midnight, so you (theoretically) fall asleep and wake up in Moscow. The best trains to Moscow are numbers 1, 3, 5 and 9. *Ploshchad Vosstaniya 2. Metro: Ploshchad Vosstaniya.*

Vitebsk Station or *Vitebsky Vokzal* serves the south Ukraine (Kiev, Odessa), Belorussia (Minsk, Brest) and Moldavia as well as Novgorod and Smolensk. There are several local trains each day to the towns of Pushkin and Pavlovsk (see *Things to See and Do: Far Out*). *Zagorodny Prospekt 52. Metro: Pushkinskaya.*

Warsaw Station or *Varshavsky Vokzal* handles trains to Lithuania, Latvia, Estonia, Lvov, Pskov, Poland and the rest of Eastern Europe, plus local trains to Gatchina. It too has a rather sleazy atmosphere and is not a safe place to hang out for any length of time. If you are travelling to Poland or beyond, it is considerably cheaper to buy a ticket to the border city of Grodno in Belorussia and then to buy a ticket for a Polish train. *Naberezhnaya Obvodnogo Kanala 118. Metro: Baltiisky Vokzal.*

Finland Station or *Finlandsky Vokzal* is the only station north of the Neva and it serves Vyborg and Helsinki. Lenin arrived here in 1917 after the February Revolution and gave a historic speech from atop an armored car. In commemoration of this speech, a statue of Lenin stands in front of the station in the aptly-named Lenin Square. In fact, your first view upon leaving the station will be Lenin's posterior.

There are two trains a day **to Helsinki**: the super fabulous Finnish *Sibelius* train which leaves in the afternoon and a morning train that is Russian and, well, Russian. Both these trains stop in Vyborg for customs. For those interested in saving a little money, take a commuter train (*elektrichka*) to Vyborg and change to a Helsinki train. Other local connections include Zelenogorsk, Sestroretsk and Repino. *Ploshchad Lenina 6. Metro: Ploshchad Lenina.*

Baltic Station or *Baltiisky Vokzal* deals exclusively with local trains to Petrodvorets, Gatchina, Lomonosov and a lot of other places far less interesting. *Naberezhnaya Obvodnogo Kanala 120. Metro: Baltiiskaya.*

Training in from Moscow
The best night trains **from Moscow** are the 2, 4, 6, 10 and 36. Advance tickets can be bought on the second floor of Moscow's **Intourtrans** office at *Ulitsa Petrovka 13/15.* The lines here are not as tortuous and the service not as atrocious as in regular ticketing agencies, though they slap on a hard currency service charge. Alternatively you can try the **Central Ticketing Office** at *Ulitsa Griboyedova 6/11,* which sells ruble tickets to all Russian and former Soviet destinations at least one day in advance. Last minute arrangements can be made at the Intourist Kassa at Moscow's **Leningrad Train Station** (*Leningradsky Vokzal*).

BY BUS

Russian buses are the automotive equivalent of *elektrichkas.* Use them as a last resort or as a disciplinary measure for unruly travelling partners. However, they may be the only possibility for travellers wishing to go directly to a city that is not serviced by trains (like Tartu in Estonia). There are two bus stations: one at *Naberezhnaya Obvodnogo Kanala 36,* a 15 minute walk from *Ligovsky Prospekt Metro* which services the Baltic countries, Novgorod, Pskov, Petrozavodsk and Vologda, and the other is at *Naberehnaya Obvodnogo Kanala 118,* located in between the

Varshavsky and Baltiisky train stations (*Metro: Baltiiskaya*) and servicing Vyborg, Lake Ladoga and other destinations to the north. Both are quite awful places to hang out after dark.

Some stylish alternatives

Express Bus has fast air-conditioned buses that run from St. Petersburg to Helsinki, Turku and Lappeenranta. They leave daily from the Pulkovskaya Hotel with stops at the Astoria, the Grand Hotel Europe and the Hotel St. Petersburg. *Non-Russians pay in hard currency. For reservations tel: 264 5125, 298 1352 (Pulkovskaya Hotel) or at the service bureaus of the abovementioned hotels.*

Finnord Bus Agency operates a line from St. Petersburg to Lahti and Helsinki with stops in Vyborg, Vaalimaa, Hamina and Kuovola. The buses depart from their office and also pick-up at the Pribaltiskaya Hotel. *Italianskaya Ulitsa 37. Metro: Gostiny Dvor. Open 10:00-17:00 daily. Non-Russians pay in hard currency. Tel: 314 8951; Fax: 314 7058.*

BY BOAT

The Main Sea Passenger Terminal is at *Ploshchad Morskoi Slavy* on the western edge of Vasilievsky Island. A currency exchange office operates when ships are in port. Satellite

communication with the outside world and other tourist services are available for passengers at Baltic Line's second floor office. Nevsky Prospekt and the city center are a 15 minute ride away and, just like the airport and train stations, there is a fleet of taxis eagerly awaiting fresh arrivals of hard currency. Alternatively, Baltic Line offers excursion buses to points all over the city.

BALTIC LINE, a Swedish shipping company, operates frequent cruise ships between Sweden, Germany, Finland and St. Petersburg. The **MS Ilich** runs year round from Stockholm to St. Petersburg. The luxurious **MS Anna Karenina** has year-round weekly voyages from Kiel, Germany, to St. Petersburg via Nynäshamn (near Stockholm). The **MS Konstantin Simonov** cruises twice a week to and from Helsinki, from early April until the end of November; the rest of the year it cruises to the Canary Islands from Morocco. The ships are modern, spacious luxury liners featuring quality restaurants, entertainment, shops, conference centers and comfortable cabins. A car deck on each ship allows passengers to bring their wheels with them.

Baltic Line arranges **tourist visas** for their round-trip passengers who also receive on-board **accommodation** in St. Petersburg, thus eliminating two of the biggest hassles involved in planning a trip to Russia. The friendly international staff will arrange guided tours and excursions, including theater tickets, and they offer a limousine service as well. Alternatively, one-way tickets are available from international destinations to St. Petersburg and vice-versa. *For bookings and information contact their representatives in the passenger terminal. Open 10:30-18:00 Mon-Fri. Tel: 355 1616; Fax: 355 6140. In Sweden tel: +46 08 520 10026; Fax: +46 8 520 12131. In Kiel tel: +49 431 982000; Fax: +49 431 9820060. In Helsinki tel: +358 0 665755; Fax: +358 0 653288. For tickets from St. Petersburg to the real world, contact the Baltic Shipping Company also in the passenger terminal, tel: 355 1312.*

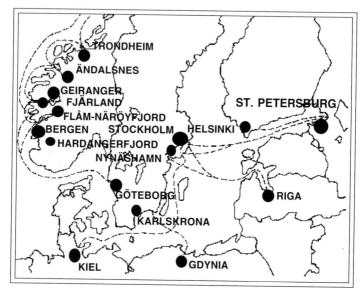

Baltic Line 1993 schedule:

Anna Karenina

Dep. Kiel	Sat	15:00	Dep. St. Petersburg	Wed	18:00
Arr. Nyhnäshamn	Sun	16:00	Arr. Nyhnäshamn	Thur	17:00
Dep. Nyhnäshamn	Sun	17:30	Dep.Nyhnäshamn	Thur	18:30
Arr. St. Petersburg	Mon	18:00	Arr. Kiel	Fri	19:30

Ilich

Dep. Riga	Wed	18:00	Dep. St. Petersburg	Mon	00:05
Arr. Stockholm	Thur	10:00	Arr. Stockholm	Tues	09:00
Dep. Stockholm	Thur	16:00	Dep. Stockholm	Tues	16:00
Arr. St. Petersburg	Fri	17:30	Arr. Riga	Wed	09:30

Konstantin Simonov

Dep. Helsinki	Mon + Thur	16:00
Arr. St. Petersburg	Tues + Fri	09:30
Dep. St. Petersburg	Thur + Sun	00:05
Arr. Helsinki	Thur + Sun	14:00

CONSULATES IN ST. PETERSBURG

Bulgaria *Ulitsa Ryleyeva 37. Metro: Chernyshevskaya. Tel: 273 4018.*

China *3th Liniya 12, Vasilievsky Island. Metro: Vasileostrovskaya. Tel: 218 1721.*

Cuba *Ulitsa Ryleyeva 37. Metro: Chernyshevskaya. Tel: 272 5303.*

Czechoslovakia *Ulitsa Tverskaya 5. Metro: Ploshchad Vosstaniya then trolley 5 or 7. Tel: 271 0459.*

Denmark *Bolshaya Alleya 13, Kamenny Ostrov. Metro: Chernaya Rechka. Tel: 234 3755.*

Finland *Ulitsa Chaikovskogo 71. Metro: Chernyshevskaya. Tel: 272 4256.*

France *Naberezhnaya Reki Moiki 15. Metro: Nevsky Prospekt. Tel: 312 1130, 314 1443.*

Germany *Ulitsa Furshtadtskaya 39. Metro: Chernyshevskaya. Tel: 273 5598.*

Great Britain *Ulitsa Proletarskoi Diktatury 5. Metro: Ploshchad Vosstaniya then trolley 5 or 7. Tel:119 6036.*

Holland *Prospekt Engelsa 101. Metro: Ozerki. Tel: 554 4900; 554 4888.*

Hungary *Ulitsa Marata 15. Metro: Mayakovskaya. Tel: 312 6458.*

Italy *Teatralnaya Ploshchad 10. Metro: Sennaya Ploshchad. Tel: 312 3217.*

Japan *Naberezhnaya Reki Moiki 29. Metro: Nevsky Prospekt. Tel: 314 1434.*

Mongolia *Leninsky Prospekt 115. Metro: Leninsky Prospekt. Tel: 153 8051.*

Poland *5th Sovetskaya Ulitsa 12. Metro: Ploshchad Vosstaniya. Tel: 274 4330.*

Sweden *10th Liniya 11, Vasilievsky Island. Metro: Vasileostrovskaya. Tel: 213 4191.*

USA *Ulitsa Furshtadtskaya 15. Metro: Chernyshevskaya. Tel: 275 1701.*

TRAVEL TO FORMER SOVIET REPUBLICS

Since visa requirements for the former Soviet Republics are still being thought up and constantly modified, anyone planning on visiting these places should either contact their own consulate or embassy for the latest visa information, or, if they don't know, try the phone numbers listed below. Be aware that with the exception of the Baltic countries it is unlikely that much English will be spoken at these Consular Offices.

The following procedures are new and will undoubtedly mutate as time goes on. As a general rule, when dealing with travel to the swarthier former republics to the south and east what the consular representative says in Moscow may be entirely different to what the border guards tell you. These guards capitalize on their fortunate assignments to make some extra money by inventing visa regulations and fees on the spot, and you can take it or leave it - a somewhat disconcerting choice for someone stranded on the Tadjik border.

Armenia: The Moscow Consulate says that a Russian Federation visa is good for now, though at the border you may hear a different story until you give a donation to the war effort. *In Moscow tel: (095) 924 1269.*

Azerbaijan: Same as Armenia, only any money taken at the border will go to the other side in the conflict. *In Moscow tel: (095) 229 1649.*

Belorussia: Visa applicants must present a tourist voucher or an official invitation to the Belorus Consulate together with photos, their passport and a visa application form. The Moscow Consulate claims that they can process a visa in one day or at the border, though it'd probably be best to play it safe and get it done in advance. *In Moscow : Ulitsa Voroseiko 17. Open 14:00-15:00 Mon-Fri. Tel: (095) 924 7095.*

Estonia: The only former republic to have a consulate in St. Petersburg. Beginning July 1, 1993, US, Canadian, British, New Zealand, Australian, Japanese and Danish citizens can travel visa free. Otherwise you'll need an invitation or tourist voucher, two photos and a visa application form. Visas are given at the border but as the night trains pull in at around 2 am and the insane hoards of people are all processed by one sleepy old lady filling everything out by hand, you're advised to do it before you go. *Bolshaya Monetnaya Ulitsa 14. Metro: Gorkovskaya. Visa applicants can submit their documents from 10:00-13:00 and receive their visas from 15:00-17:00 on Tues and Fri. Tel: 233 5548.*

Georgia: For the time being a Russian visa will get you in though the Consul openly admitted that the people working the border may have some other opinion on this matter. *In Moscow tel: (095) 290 6902.*

Kazakhstan: Visas are given only with an invitation and take two weeks to process. *In Moscow tel: (095) 208 3775.*

Kirghistan: A Russian visa will get you in. *In Moscow tel: (095) 237 4481.*

Latvia: British, Polish and Hungarian citizens can travel here visa-free. Everyone else can receive a visa on the border or in the airport by filling out the application form and providing one passport-size photo. *In Moscow: Ulitsa Chapygina 3. US citizens receive visas free of charge. Tel: (095) 925 2703.*

Lithuania: British citizens travel visa-free. Otherwise similar to the Latvian visa procedure. *In Moscow: Ulitsa Pisemskogo 10. Tel: (095) 291 2643.*

Moldova: Visas available (by invitation except for transit visas) at the border or airport, and in Moscow. *In Moscow tel: (095) 924 5546.*

Tadjikistan: They claim that a Russian visa is good, though this may change soon. If it does, you can always try to get one at the border...*In Moscow tel: (095) 290 5736.*

Turkmenistan: Visas available in Moscow; the border situation is unclear. *In Moscow tel: (095) 291 6591, 291 6636.*

Ukraine: You'll need to fill out visa forms at one of their Consulates. It takes a couple of days to process and they'll need photos and money. They offer huge discounts to students studying in the former USSR. *In Moscow: Ulitsa Stanislavskogo 18. Open 10:00-12:00 Mon-Fri. Tel: (095) 229 6475.*

Uzbekistan: According to the Embassy, visas are not given at the border, though not to hear the corrupt border guards tell it. The Embassy will issue a visa in a day if you provide them with an invitation, photos and money; "how about $50?" *In Moscow: Pogorelsky Pereulok 12. Tel: (095) 230 1301.*

DOING BUSINESS IN RUSSIA?

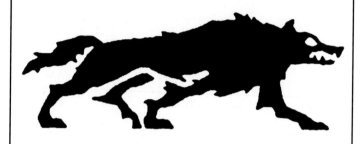

*then keep in mind that in Russia
professional security will save you money.*

*For long term security arrangements provided by
a no-nonsense and established American
company employing highly qualified and
disciplined personnel.*

SGC INTERNATIONAL, INC.

TELEPHONE:	**+7 812 234 0844**
FAX:	**+7 812 234 1266**
TELEX:	**121 737**

SAFETY WARNINGS

"The city streets are really quite a thrill,
If the hoods don't get you the monoxide will."
- Tom Lehrer

S AFETY ISSUES IN RUSSIA get a lot of press. In 1992, *Newsweek* featured a story that compared St. Petersburg with 1930s Chicago, plus every time there is a nuclear accident the Western press rushes to compare it to Chernobyl. In addition, there is a lot of coverage dedicated to Communism's ruinous effects on the environment. Based on all these reports you might expect to see drive-by shootings by blind mutants with black lungs and chronic diarrhoea.

Petersburg can be a dangerous place. Of course Helsinki can be dangerous too if you step in front of a runaway cement truck. The reality is that crime is no worse than in other cities of similar size and it's no more polluted here than Bombay, Katowice or Los Angeles. Petersburg is home to over 5 million people and all the problems of big cities everywhere can be found here. There's no need to be paranoid, but it helps to be aware.

HEALTH WARNINGS

The Water

"Lots of things there that you can drink,
But stay away from the kitchen sink"

Actually the term "water" may not be the most accurate description of the liquid that comes out of taps, but for want of a better word it will have to suffice. You'll know what we mean when you pour yourself a large glass or fill some container (a bathtub, for instance) with the fluid - it's not quite as transparent as one would like, especially the stuff that comes from the hot water pipes. Mendeleev probably made his pioneering discovery of the Periodic Table of Elements after examining a glass of it.

The water is drawn from Lake Ladoga and the Neva River where large collective farms and heavy industries dump their waste. Large amounts of chlorine, added to the water supply to kill off the bacteria from the animal waste, react with the heavier elements from the industrial dumping. In a word, the water is pretty heinous.

But wait, there's more... Even worse than the various heavy metals and industrial pollutants in the water is the little parasite called *giardia lamblia*, which causes a most unpleasant disease (see *Medical* for more gruesome specifics). You should definitely avoid drinking untreated water, though it is impossible to avoid all contact with untreated or unboiled water as dishes are washed in it, you will probably bathe in it, vegetables are (hopefully) cleaned with it and so on. Act on the things you have control over and with everything else just hope for the best.

Water Tips

- Boil water for at least 5 minutes before drinking it;

- If you plan on staying in Petersburg for any substantial period of time, some purifying tablets or a purifying pump with an anti-microbial filter are very good investments;

- Bring some metronidazole with you in case you come down with giardia and the hard currency pharmacies are out;

- If you have goldfish you'll need to let the water sit open for a couple of days to de-chlorinate before pouring it into the aquarium or the little fishies will be floating upside down in no time;

- If you have sensitive skin (and even if you don't) bring along some skin cream as the water has a drying effect.

- Be wary of some juice drinks that are made of concentrate and water, as the latter may not be purified.

Insane Drivers
It won't take you too long to figure this one out yourself. Drivers will cruise the wrong side of the road, drive in reverse down major streets, or even navigate the sidewalk on occasion. Don't take anything for granted - local drivers treat one-way streets, traffic lights and the sanctity of crosswalks as suggestions rather than laws. People swerve at 80 km/h attempting to avoid the billions of potholes that dot the streets like bad acne. Look both ways, look again, hold your breath and run. Always take an underground crossing (переход) if you can.

ENVIRONMENTAL CONCERNS

*"Just go out for a breath of air,
And you'll be ready for Medicare"*

To get an idea of why the air quality is not so wonderful here, stand on a street that has a lot of bus and truck traffic and watch the huge billows of pungent black smoke belching from gargantuan tailpipes. Sixty percent of air pollution comes from transport, a scary statistic if you've ever seen the other forty percent pouring out of industrial smokestacks. Nevertheless it never gets to the point where it is downright dangerous to go outside without a gas mask; most likely the worst thing that will happen is that a bus will drive by and gush exhaust in your face and make your clothes smell.

According to recent readings, **background radiation** in St. Petersburg corresponds to international norms. The closest nuclear power plant is in Sosnovy Bor, 70 kilometers west of St. Petersburg. The power plant works quite well, though it is the same design as the better-known Chernobyl reactor and is even slightly older. If this thing blows you should take cover - in Argentina.

CRIME

The face of crime has changed quite a lot in Russia over the last decade. Whereas 10 years ago the Russian police force spent a good deal of energy pursuing people in possession of illicit copies of Dr. Zhivago and harassing young men with long hair, nowadays they have real criminals to deal with. That's not to say that before *perestroika* there were no rapes, knifings, robberies and so on, but these were so infrequent that the average person didn't think much about them at all. Now all you hear from Russians are stories about how dangerous it is for foreigners to walk alone anywhere after dark, to speak English in public, to take taxis, to buy bread...

The reality is that St. Petersburgers are being faced with what people from London, New York, Rome and other large cities have faced for a long time, and it will take a while for them to get used to it. There is no rule that says all foreigners will be mercilessly picked out of a crowd, beaten up and robbed, at least not yet. Use you head, keep your voice down and there shouldn't be any problems.

Theft

The most common crime is **pickpocketing**. Watch your valuables on all forms of public transport and in touristy places where there are large crowds, for instance in train stations, on Nevsky Prospekt (especially between Kanal Griboyedova and Sadovaya Ulitsa) and around St. Isaac's Cathedral. Gypsy kids and moms pull the same heists that they do everywhere; crowding around, grabbing and tugging and looking pitiful while their little hands magically remove all your valuables.

Unfortunately **armed robberies** are also on the rise. Most of these involve knives but guns are becoming more and more commonplace. These crimes usually occur when the victim is alone in an isolated place (courtyard, park, small alley, etc.), though they can happen in broad daylight in front of passersby who don't want to get involved. The best advice is to be a little wary of trumpeting your status as a foreigner anytime you're not with a good-sized group.

If you have been pickpocketed then there's not too much you can do about it. If you should become the victim of a robbery, however, you should report it to the police. **The militia phone number is 02**. You'll need a translator as they rarely have English speakers on duty. Of course try to remember as many details about the perpetrators as possible, including clothing, descriptive markings and whether they spoke Russian, French or some other language.

The most important thing is not to be paranoid. At the same time be aware that the crime rate is rising and that criminals naturally go after people that they suspect have money. No place is 100% safe and no place is 100% dangerous. Keep your head on straight whether on the street, in a bus or in a disco. Careless behavior will only make potential thieves' jobs much easier.

A Word on Organized Crime
Considering that Russia was run by organized criminals for 74 years, it should not come as much of a surprise that this type of activity flourishes here. Tourists are unlikely to come into direct contact with organized criminals and should be more concerned about small random acts on the part of drunks, thugs and thieves. On the other hand, anyone who wants to do business here will most likely have to confront the organized crime problem. This book is not the place for an in-depth discussion of mafia issues; the most reasonable advice we can give is for you to talk to members of the foreign business community who have been here for a while and theoretically know the ropes.

LANGUAGE

ONE OF THE MOST OBVIOUS problems a visitor to Russia will face is the language barrier. Unlike those simple European languages such as Hungarian and Latin, Russian is not a language you can just pick up after hearing it for a few days. To those unfamiliar with it, Russian seems intimidating and just getting used to the funky letters can be a real pain in the жопа.

A lot of people in St. Petersburg have studied English. A lot of them have also studied Marxism-Leninism. The textbooks, by an amazing coincidence, are quite similar - schoolchildren became acquainted with the English language by reading about the wild and wacky adventures of V.I. Lenin in London, the history of the Young Communist League, snippets from <u>Ten Days that Shook the World</u> and other classics of the English language. Most students also had to contend with a complete lack of practice, leading most people to forget what they learned the way we've all forgotten trigonometry. Besides, the Soviet Ministry of Education, like most Soviet ministries, concerned itself more with cranking out loyal citizens than with producing people able to communicate freely with Western imperialists. Thus although many people have a passive knowledge of English and may know some basic words, it is rare to find a person with conversational fluency. Times are of course rapidly changing and English is all the rage, particularly with the younger generation.

It is even more uncommon to find people with active knowledge of another European language. German is the most common of the uncommon, thanks to the inclusion of the German Democratic Republic in the happy Socialist camp; but to find a Spanish, French or Finnish speaker is quite rare. In the business community people are more likely to know some foreign language (usually English) or else have translators readily at hand, but once out of this environment, it's a lot of "I'm sorry, do you want buy military watch?" and "Hello my name is two hundred dollars."

Speaking Russian

When off the beaten tourist track non-Russian speakers will find it difficult to communicate even their most basic needs and desires. Busy shop clerks, devious taxi drivers and surly waiters may have little tolerance for those who haven't spent years developing their Russian language ability. On the other hand, when in a social environment, any effort on your part to speak Russian will serve not only to break the ice but will also help the listener to feel more relaxed about trying to speak your language. You will constantly hear apologies from Russians for their pronunciation and vocabulary, even if they are quite conversational in your language. Always be reassuring, though don't correct them unless they specifically ask you to (many will). When speaking English to Russians, be aware that modesty may keep them from asking you to repeat something that they felt they should have understood the first time.

RUSSIAN LESSONS HERE

There are several organizations that teach Russian to foreigners.

University Center for Russian Language and Culture has courses ranging from one week to one year, in groups of 5 to 8 or individually. These guys have been teaching Russian language enthusiasts since 1960, and many universities give credit for time done here. Payment is in sizeable amounts of hard currency. *Universitetskaya Naberezhnaya 7/9. Metro: Nevsky Prospekt then trolley 1. Tel: 218 9452; Fax: 218 1346; Telex 121 481 LSU SU.*

Aslantis offers programs that cater to all levels from beginning conversational to intensive, with special lectures in literature, history, politics, business and/or social sciences available. They can arrange accommodation with a family or in a private apartment. Study groups are small (usually three or less people) and programs can be individually designed with more informal interests (music, art, nightlife) emphasized if desired. *P.O. Box 398, St. Petersburg 196105. Tel/Fax: 298 9007.*

The Gertsen University Individual or group courses for all levels from one month to several years, also for sizeable amounts of hard currency. *Ulitsa Plekhanova 6. Metro: Nevsky Prospekt. Tel: 314 7668, 314 7773 (English); Fax: 314 7859.*

Vneshvuz Center In addition to group and individual courses, they teach "Survival Russian" and "Business Russian" (note how the two are separate courses). They also provide cultural programs and can arrange accommodation. *Morskaya Naberezhnaya 9. Metro: Primorskaya. Tel: 356 9905, 101 3283 (English).*

THE RUSSIAN ALPHABET

Cyrillic	Transliteration	Sounds like*
Аа	A	"A" in Jaws
Бб	B	"B" in Bozo
Вв	V	"V" in Venom
Гг	G	"G" in Grits
Дд	D	"D" in Deportation
Ее	E or Ye	"Ye" in Yeltsin
Ёё	Yo	"Yo" in Yo dude!
Жж	Zh	"G" in Massage
Зз	Z	"Z" in Zulu warrior
Ии	I	"Ee" in Cheese
Йй	Y (or J)	"Y" in Yuppie[1]
Кк	K	"K" in Kitsch
Лл	L	"L" in Leprosy
Мм	M	"M" in Mange
Нн	N	"N" in Nappy
Оо	O	"O" in Broke
Пп	P	"P" in Prince Charles
Рр	R	"R" in Randy Andy
Сс	S	"S" in Superman
Тт	T	"T" in Pterodactyl
Уу	U	"Oo" in Winnie the Pooh
Фф	F	"F" in Funky
Хх	Kh	Kh[2]
Цц	Ts	"Ts" in Tse Tse fly
Чч	Ch	"Ch" in Chimpanzee
Шш	Sh	"Sh" in Shakedown
Щщ	Shch	Sh[3]
Ъъ	unpronounced	hard sign[4]
Ыы	Y	I[5]
Ьь	unpronounced	soft sign[6]
Ээ	E	"E" in Eggs Benedict
Юю	Yu	"U" in Useless
Яя	Ya	"Ya" in Yahoo

---

* The words we give to illustrate similarities in sound are valid only if pronounced with an American accent. Fresh Air cannot assume responsibility for negative results from misuse of the Bungy System by people speaking with a British or Australian accent, or any other dialect of American.

[1] This letter mostly occurs at the end of words where it is not pronounced.

Fresh Tip: First and foremost learn the alphabet. For some of the stranger looking letters it can be useful to think up associations (for instance, the flying bug is a "Ж", the spaceship a "Ю", etc.). Once you get over the more confusing aspects of Cyrillic letters it becomes quite easy to read individual words.

SOME VERY BASIC RUSSIAN[7]

DO YOU SPEAK ENGLISH?
Vy gava<u>ree</u>tye po-an<u>glee</u>ski?
Вы говорите по — английски?

I DON'T SPEAK RUSSIAN.
Ya ne gavar<u>yoo</u> po-<u>roo</u>sski.
Я не говорю по — русский.

---

[2]To make this sound you need to press the rear of your tongue to the roof of your mouth and expel air in a snake-like hiss. It may help to imagine a cat coughing up hair balls. Other languages that use this sound include Polish, Hebrew and Arabic.

[3]Similar to the Ш sound, though "softer." No need to lose any sleep over the difference.

[4]The hard sign used to be at the end of every word that ended in a consonant in pre-Revolutionary texts; nowadays it is rather insignificant.

[5]The "hard vowel" complement to И has no English equivalent; it is essentially an "ee" sound pronounced from the back of the throat.

[6]The soft sign appears at the end of all infinitive verbs and in many words. It does wonderful things to the letter preceeding it, and is an eternal nightmare for students of Russian phonetics.

[7]The transliterations do not correspond to the Library of Congress system most commonly used in America, or to other systems used. These systems are useful for reading and indexing, but as a pronunciation guide they will only cause laughter and merriment amongst the listeners. The Bungy Method, though it looks funny, gives a more accurate idea of how the words should be pronounced. Accented syllables are underlined. Note that the unstressed "o" in Russian is pronounced "ah". The unstressed "e" is pronounced like the "и" (ee). In this transliterated system, a "y" breaks up a vowel cluster into distinctly pronounced syllables, so that "aye" is pronounced "ah-yeh".

Hello .... *Zdrastvuitye* .... Здрасвтвуйте
Goodbye .... *Do svidanya* .... До свидания
Thank you .... *Spaseeba* .... Спасибо
Please,
You're welcome .... *Pazhalsta* .... Пожалуйста
I'm sorry,
Excuse me .... *Izvineetye* .... Извините
Yes .... *Da* .... Да
No .... *Nyet* .... Нет
Good .... *Kharasho* .... Хорошо
Bad .... *Plokha* .... Плохо
Maybe .... *Mozhet byt* .... Может быть
Hi (informal) .... *Privyet* .... Привет
Bye (informal) .... *Paka* .... Пока
Help! .... *Pamageetye!* .... Помогите!

CAFE AND RESTAURANT TALK

Cafe .... *Kafe* .... Кафе
Restaurant .... *Restaran* .... Ресторан
Please bring me .... *Prineseetye pazhalsta* ...... Принесите
                                                                                             пожалуйста
  the bill .... *Schot* .... Счёт
  an ashtray .... *pepelneetsu* .... пепельницу
  more vodka .... *yeshcho vodki* .... ещё водки
I would like..................... *Ya khachoo* .... Я хочу
  a salad .... *salat* .... салат
  a bottle of port wine ..... *butylku partvehna* ...... бутылку портвейна
Keep the change .... *Astavtye zdachu sebye* .... Оставьте сдачу себе
Can I pay .... *Mozhna plateet* .... Можно платить
  In cash .... *naleechnimi* .... наличными
  By credit card .... *kredeetnoi kartachkoi* .. кредитной карточкой
I want to speak to the .... *Pazaveetye, pazhalsta* ..... Позовите пожалуйста
  manager .... *menedzhera* .... менеджера
  head waiter .... *starsheva ofitsyanta* .... старшего официанта
  cook.............................. *povara* .... повара
Do you charge by   *U vas aplata*   У вас оплата
the hour? .... *pachasavaya?* .... почасовая?

ON THE STREET

Where is	*Gdye*	Где
the metro	*metro*	метро
the hotel	*gasteenitsa*	гостиница
How can I get to	*Kak dayekhat do*	Как доехать до
Shove off!	*Atvalee*	Отвали
Where am I?	*Gdye ya nakhazhoos?*	Где я нахожусь?
Does your dog bite?	*Vasha sabaka ni kusayetsa?*	Ваша собака не кусается?

SHOPPING

How much?	*Skolka stoyit*	Сколько стоит
It's too expensive	*Eta doraga*	Это дорого
I only have rubles	*U menya tolka rublee*	У меня только рубли
In rubles	*V rublyakh*	В рублях
In dollars	*V dollarakh*	В долларах
May I look at	*Pakazheetye, pazhalsta*	Покажите пожалуйста
that book	*etu kneegu*	эту книгу
I'll take this	*Ya eto vazmoo*	Я это возьму
Two kilos of rhubarb, please	*Dva kilograma revenya, pazhalsta*	Два килограма ревеня, пожалуйста

IN A TAXI

Left	*Naleva*	Налево
Right	*Naprava*	Направо
Straight	*Pryama*	Прямо
Please stop here	*Astanaveetes pazhalsta*	Остановитесь, пожалуйста
Wait for me here	*Padazhdeetye menya, pazhalsta*	Подождите меня, пожалуйста
Why are you driving on the sidewalk?	*Zachem vy yeditye po tratuaru?*	Зачем вы едете по тротуару?

NUMBERS

0	*nol*	нол
1	*adeen*	один
2	*dva*	два
3	*tri*	три
4	*cheteeri*	четыре
5	*pyat*	пять
6	*shest*	шесть
7	*syem*	семь
8	*vosyem*	восемь
9	*devyit*	девять
10	*desyit*	десять
11	*adeenatsat*	одиннадцать
12	*dvenatsat*	двенадцать
13	*trinatsat*	тринадцать
14	*cheteernatsat*	четырнадцать
15	*pitnatsat*	пятнадцать
16	*shestnatsat*	шестнадцать
17	*semnatsat*	семнадцать
18	*vosemnatsat*	восемнадцать
19	*devitnatsat*	девятнадцать
20	*dvatsat*	двадцать
30	*treetsat*	тридцать
40	*sorok*	сорок
50	*pitdesyat*	пятьдесят
60	*shestdesyat*	шестьдесят
70	*semdesyat*	семьдесят
80	*vosemdesyat*	восемьдесят
90	*devinosta*	девяносто
100	*sto*	сто
200	*dvesti*	двести
300	*treesta*	триста
400	*cheteeresta*	четыреста
500	*pitsot*	пятьсот
1,000	*teesicha*	тысяча
5,000	*pyat teesich*	пят тысяч
10,000	*desit teesich*	десять тысяч
100,000	*sto teesich*	сто тысяч
1,000,000	*milliyon*	миллион

MONEY

THE DYNAMIC AND TURBULENT changes that Russia is experiencing are no more evident than when dealing with the money. For the past few years the ruble has been doing something akin to going over Niagara Falls in a barrel. Runaway inflation and lack of confidence in the rascally ruble has led most people to treat US dollars as a second, if not first currency. Most of the former Republics have adopted their own currencies (the Belorussians winning the award for the most non-provocative money, covering it with cute little bunny rabbits and squirrels), and printing presses are working overtime as Russia gets flooded with more worthless bits of colored paper.

To make matters more confusing there are two varieties of rubles in circulation at the moment, both equally valid. The first kind is the old Soviet ruble, recognizable by the CCCP written on them and Lenin's profile on bills of 10 or larger. Soviet rubles come in denominations of 1, 3, 5, 10, 25, 50, 100, 200, 500, 1000 and 5000 (the last having no Lenin on it), and there are 1, 5 and 10 ruble coins as well. These rubles are divisible into 100 kopecks. Although kopecks are absolutely worthless and almost completely obsolete, the 15 kopeck coin is still used in public pay phones that haven't yet been converted to take metro tokens.

The Russian Federation, heir to a vast fortune of Soviet rubles dumped by the former republics, has begun printing rubles of its own. These come in denominations of 100, 200, 500, 1000, 5000 and 10000, and expect more zeroes in the near future. There are also Russian Federation coins in denominations of 10, 20, 50 and 100 in circulation, recognizable by the two-headed symbol on their reverse side. Needless to say there are no Lenins on the new money and the only indication of the country's socialist past to be garnered from these colorful new rubles is their intrinsic worthlessness.

Bringing Money into the Country

For reasons best left to financial analysts and shotgun toting red-necks, **US dollars** are the most favored currency in those Russian cities that have foreign money flowing through them. This phenomenon is reflected in pricing policies, demand on the black market, and any time a discussion about money takes place. Banks and black marketeers alike give the highest relative exchange rate to dollars, so it is the best currency to bring. Banks will change most major Western currencies into rubles, although many hard currency hotels, stores and restaurants take only US dollars, deutschmarks, Swedish kroner and Finnish marks as these are the most common currencies here. In addition, not too many establishments accept travellers cheques or credit cards (hotels are the main exception), so you may be forced to tote around large amounts of cash. It is useful to have money in small denominations as sometimes it can be hard to find change for big ones.

How Much to Bring

It is difficult to say how much money one should bring to Russia, as it depends on so many factors most importantly your choice of life-style. If you try to stick to a ruble only life-style, Russia can be unbelievably cheap; thus a massive conspiracy has formed amongst everyone you deal with to try to keep this from being exploited. Besides, the pure ruble life is a serious drag. Given that you will have a certain amount of currency expenditures, keep in mind that Russia is a place more oriented on cash than on credit cards and travellers cheques. The most expensive things (hotels, fancy restaurants, rental cars) can be put on credit cards, so although if you run out of cash you won't be forced to roam the streets and live under bridges, you may find upon leaving that your credit card bill has exceeded the Gross National Product of Bolivia.

Currency Services*

American Express has a fully functioning office in the Grand Hotel Europe which sells cheques to cardholders, changes money, replaces lost or stolen cards, cashes travellers cheques and provides information on local establishments that accept the American Express Card. *Mikhailovskaya Ulitsa 1/7. Metro: Nevsky Prospekt. The travel department will accept all major credit cards. Open 09:00-17:00 Mon-Fri. Tel: 119 6009; Fax: 119 6011.*

American Express, Visa, Master Card, Citicorp and Bank of America travellers cheques can also be cashed across the street from the American Express office at **Industry and Construction Bank**. *Nevsky Prospekt 38 (entry from Mikhailovskaya Ulitsa). Metro: Nevsky Prospekt. Open 09:30-18:30 Mon-Sat.*

Cash advances can be made against a Visa Card through **St. Petersburg Savings Bank**. *Nevsky Prospekt 38 (entry from Mikhailovskaya Ulitsa). Metro: Nevsky Prospekt. Open 10:00-18:00 Mon-Sat. Tel: 110 4945. Also on the 1st floor of the Hotel Pulkovskaya, Ploshchad Pobedy 2. Metro: Moskovskaya. Open 09:00-21:00 daily. Tel: 264 5147.*

BANKING: FINANCIAL RUSSIAN ROULETTE

Another way to receive money is by **wire transfer**. To do this, pick a local commercial bank and have the sum wired to one of their foreign correspondent banks. After processing, you will be able to receive the cash at the bank here. In addition to

---

*Whenever receiving money by bank transfer, cash advance or travellers cheque purchase, be sure that you get a *razreshenie* (разрешение) form which you should keep together with your **customs declaration**. This form serves as an addendum to the declaration, increasing the amount of money brought into the country and therefore the amount that can be taken back out again.

taking transfer fees, the majority of Russian banks require that you open a personal hard currency account in order for you to withdraw the money (for this they naturally charge a fee). The transfer usually takes three to four days to clear although this could speed up considerably if more banks get on the SWIFT system (an international network of well-trained carrier pigeons and homing badgers). Hard currency, like shoes and cheese, is in great demand so don't be surprised if you go to pick up your transfer at the bank and they've run out of everything except Spanish pesetas and Lebanese pounds. Few banks have foreign-language staff working as tellers, though they do usually have workers in the building who in a pinch can act as translators.

Russian Trade & Industry Bank offers transfer services to non-account holders. *Ulitsa Gertsena 15. Metro: Nevsky Prospekt. Open 09:00-12:30 Mon-Fri, currency exchange open until 18:00. Tel: 315 7833; Fax: 311 2135.*

Industry & Construction Bank *Nevsky Prospekt 38. Metro: Nevsky Prospekt. Open 09:30-12:30 Mon-Fri, currency exchange open until 18:00.*

Credobank *Mokhovaya Ulitsa 26. 15 minutes from Metros Gostiny Dvor and Chernyshevskaya. Open 09:30-13:00 (currency exchange open 10:00-12:00). Tel: 275 0333; Fax: 275 0331.*

CHANGING MONEY

You have a choice of how to change money: you can do it legally through a currency exchange booth or bank, or illegally on the black market. Almost everyone has shaken off the psychological restraints caused by old laws that could jail a person for possession of foreign currency, and there are plenty of people out there willing to give you rubles in either an official or unofficial capacity. More often than not the black market is more convenient and offers a better rate, though it entails some element of risk. Plus there is the moral issue of which type of criminals you choose to support - currency speculators or government bureaucrat stooges.

Whenever you hand hard currency over to someone it is quite common for the bills to be individually checked for authenticity either with some electronic device of questionable effectiveness or by a bizarre variety of techniques including rubbing, crumpling, ripping and tasting. Don't take this as an insult as counterfeit money has proliferated in this country during the last couple of years. Torn, well worn and faded money almost always gets turned down here.

The Legal Way

A number of commercial banks have set up exchange points throughout the city. Rates are usually just slightly lower than the better black market offerings, though different banks have different rates. In general, the more touristy the location (like the Hermitage, *Dom Knigi* and near major hotels), the lower the rate, though the difference is usually negligible. Watch for crafty commission rules that make changing small amounts completely pointless. You will be given a slip recording the transaction which you should keep with your **customs declaration** just in case some anal-retentive customs officer decides to actually check how much money you are taking out.

Re-converting

It is against Russian Federation law to export rubles (wait for laughter to subside). Reconversion of unspent rubles to hard currency can theoretically be accomplished at the airport, port authority or border. You'll need your customs declaration, receipts from money-changing transactions, any разрешения forms you may have and don't be surprised if they ask for proof of purchase seals, used tram tickets and a note from your parents. The most likely scenario is that they will tell you they have no currency and confiscate your rubles "for safe keeping", giving you a receipt to allow you to pick them up the next time you come into the country. Of course by that time the rate will either be a zillion to one or a presidential decree will have made dried birds nests the official currency.

You can also reconvert rubles on the black market or in banks although it's really only worth the trouble if you somehow ended up with bags of the stuff. Just spend them, smuggle them out as souvenirs or give them to someone who needs them more than you (our address is in the front of the book).

The Less Legal Way

Hard currency can still be bought and sold on the **black market** here. It's pretty easy to spot the black marketeers as they stand around holding small cards that say $, FM, DM and whatever other currencies they take. Many of them lurk around metro stations, major tourist sights and in front of currency exchange offices. Some kiosks dabble in the exchange business (these hang the abovementioned cards in their windows). Though black market activity is illegal and perpetrators on both sides occasionally get detained by police, most often officials look askance at it (at least for the moment) and your biggest concern should not be the legality of the transaction but the scruples of the person you are changing money with.

As with the black market anywhere, many of the people involved are rip-off artists. The ones who specialize in foreigners (you'll know who they are by their good street English and their privileged turf) are the most suspect. Some are particularly good at sleight-of-hand, miraculously transforming one-hundred dollar bills into ones or a stack of 5000 ruble notes into a pile of Polish zloty. Some work in teams, with one or more people distracting you while someone quietly performs a complete cashectomy on you. A select few will just punch you in the mouth or point knives and guns in your general direction. Nevertheless, for the most part the changers are just trying to make an honest living (well maybe it's not so honest) and usually the worst they will do is give you a crappy rate.

There are a few do's and don'ts that anyone changing money on the black market should keep in mind.

DO:

- be wary of large groups of people taking part in the transaction. A lot of other changers standing around minding their own business generally is a good sign as it means the place is a major currency market. But when a lot of people gather round and all of them are talking, pointing, pushing and rummaging through your pockets, you are probably on the road to a set-up;

- make sure you have examined the stack of rubles before you hand over your currency. Check to see they are indeed rubles and that there aren't any torn bills. One common scam is when the black marketeer gives you just under the agreed amount and when you point this out he takes the money back, counts out the missing amount and gives it back to you. What you most likely did not notice was that he switched stacks (leaving you with a bunch of near-worthless bills) or performed a crafty and popular sleight-of-hand trick, folding most of the money back into his hand. Such rip-offs are usually concluded by the black marketeer exclaiming in a panic "look out, it's the KGB!" and doing a quick disappearing act. Such behavior is a sure-fire indication that you have just been Jonesed;

- think quickly if the black marketeer tries to cancel the exchange mid-way through after he has already handled your currency. After the quickly orchestrated cancellation which ends with the black marketeer making an escape, you will notice that the folded hundred dollar bill he handed back to you is now a one. Sometimes con-artists go through incredulous theatricals to accomplish this scam, including the use of dramatic timing and stampeding goats.

DON'T:

- be afraid to walk out on a transaction midway through. If surrounding people start acting suspiciously you are almost definitely in the process of being chumped. Best to just go away and live to change money another way;

- step into someone's car or kiosk. They call the shots in their territory;

- make the mistake of thinking that some of these punks won't kill you for a hundred bucks;

- say we didn't warn you.

Really, most often everything goes smoothly and to the mutual benefit of both sides.

Many people who work in places that deal in hard currency will not be above offering to change money for you. Hotel doormen, restaurant waiters and people who work in stores where there are official currency exchange booths may do a little currency trading of their own. These are usually safe options as since you know where they work they are less likely to rip you off.

Final Words o' Wisdom

Large bills in both rubles and currency can be hard to get change for. Trying to buy a metro token with a 10000 ruble bill will result in some snappy comments from the cashier and no token for you. The same usually goes for buying a can of beer with a hundred dollar bill. You will be amazed at a country where money is being thrown around everywhere and yet nobody has any change.

Almost every currency establishment will accept rubles as payment and many ruble enterprises will be glad to take hard currency. It is always a good idea to have at least several dollars worth of rubles as many places that have inflated prices for foreigners (like museums) may only take rubles. There will almost always be a way to get more rubles, but just when you need them most you won't find any or you'll get pooched on the rate.

ACCOMMODATION

A FEW YEARS AGO A VISITOR arriving in St. Petersburg was not given a choice of where to stay. Hapless victims of the Soviet tourist monopoly were hauled off to their 'lodgings', usually a drab concrete block filled with miserable service and inedible food, and the only people who paid any attention to them were the local KGB spooks. Nowadays things are quite different. A number of joint venture and private hotels have opened and a good dose of market competition has forced even the drabbest of concrete monstrosities to upgrade their service. Most hotels competing for international clientele understand that to remain in the market they must provide adequate facilities and treat visitors as guests rather than *gulag* inmates.

With the exception of the major international hotels, prices can vary according to the guest's nationality. This means that next door to your $200 a night suite you may find some Muscovites paying only 20,000 rubles for an identical room. Attempts to argue this point with receptionists, managers and staff in Soviet-style hotels will at best result in a blank stare and a shrug of the shoulders, or at worst a sharp diatribe about the average salary of postal workers and whatnot in your country as compared to here. Becoming indignant won't help as this type of price discrimination is the only way many hotels can remain affordable to travelling postal workers and the like.

Russian Hotels
Most Russian-run hotels still operate on the old system whereby you must trade your room key for a hotel card with the *dezhurnaya*, or floor attendant (usually an elderly *babushka*), whenever you leave your floor. She may also take care of laundry, provide tea (for a price) and chase away visitors she sees as unwanted. You will be expected to leave your **visa and**

passport with the reception desk for registration purposes. Some hotel tariffs include meals, though usually only breakfast, and any other meals taken in the hotel are charged separately. The word "deluxe" gets haphazardly thrown around in advertisements for former Intourist hotels which can sometimes be misleading. Be prepared for periodic hot-water shutdowns, broken appliances, poor maid service and a generally lower standard of everything in these hotels. There are, of course, exceptions and they are listed below.

Local telephone calls from your hotel room are free and calls to Moscow and other places in the former Soviet Union aren't too expensive. If the hotel does not have direct international phone access either from the rooms or from special phones in the lobby, then they can book long distance calls for you. International calls from major hotels are always much more expensive than placing the call yourself; it pays to check out the rates before dialing (see *Communicating with the Outside World* for details on placing international calls).

The Service Bureau
Hotel service bureaus can take care of most tourist needs for guests and non-guests alike. They can arrange car rentals, guided tours and excursions as well as theater tickets and restaurant reservations. Some sell train tickets and can make airline bookings. Of course it will always be cheaper to do these things yourself but since making these arrangements is usually a royal pain in the tuckus, using a service bureau can be quite convenient.

INTERNATIONAL STANDARD

NEVSKIJ PALACE HOTEL is a new five-star deluxe hotel run by the Austrian company Marco Polo Hotels and Resorts. Located in the center of St. Petersburg on the city's main thoroughfare, the Palace Hotel has 287 rooms exquisitely renovated and offers its guests an extensive range of services including a secure parking garage under the hotel, international communications and business facilities, conference rooms and a fitness center. A covered arcade with international quality shops, fine restaurants, cafes and bars have created a much-needed center for tourism and business in the heart of the city. *Nevsky Prospekt 57. Metro: Mayakovskaya. Reservations through all major travel agents and any computerized reservations system. Major credit cards accepted. St. Petersburg tel: 275 2001; Fax: 113 1470; Telex: +64 121279 HERMS SU. By satellite tel: 850 1500; Fax: 850 1501.*

ASTORIA Located in one of the most beautiful parts of St. Petersburg's historic center, St. Isaac's Square, the recently renovated Astoria boasts a wide range of top-quality services and amenities. Rooms are large and comfortable and the overall feeling of elegance makes this one of the best hotels in St. Petersburg. Its restaurants and bars are popular with guests and residents from all around the city and there is a business center, several shops, international phone lines, a sauna and health club, a full range of tourist services from tickets to guided tours, and a guarded parking lot. *Ulitsa Gertsena 39. Metro: Nevsky Prospect. Hard currency or rubles. Major credit cards accepted. Reception: 210 5010, 210 5020, 315 9676; Service bureau: 210 5045; Fax: 315 9668; Telex: 121213 ASTOR SU.*

GRAND HOTEL EUROPE A joint venture between RESO Hotels, SIAB Construction and the City of St. Petersburg, the five-star Grand Hotel has been painstakingly restored to the opulence of its turn-of-the-century heyday. The level of service is quite high and the hotel has business facilities and features several high-class restaurants and bars. *Mikhailovskaya Ulitsa 1/7. Metro: Nevsky Prospekt. Major credit cards accepted. Reservations: USA 1-800-THE-OMNI, UK 071 937 8033, Sweden 08 23 47 00, Finland 90 13 1001. St. Petersburg tel: 119 6000; Fax: 119 6001; Telex: +64 121073.*

OLYMPIA A RESO joint venture hotelship moored near the Main Sea Passenger Terminal next to the Lenexpo Exhibition Center on Vasilievsky Island, the Olympia features the open-air "White Nights" Bar from May to September and the usual high standard of service provided by RESO hotels worldwide. *Ploshchad Morskoi Slavy 1. Major credit cards accepted. Tel: 119 6800; Fax: 119 6805; Telex: +64 121333; By satellite: 873 137 0316; Fax: 873 137 0317.*

PRIBALTISKAYA This huge imposing hotel on the Gulf of Finland has a comprehensive list of amenities including a business and conference center, Petersburg's only bowling alley, a Baltic Star hard currency shop and a full service bureau. Many of the rooms have a great view over the Gulf, and there are special rooms for disabled travellers. *Ulitsa Korablestroitelei 14, Vasilievsky Island. Metro: Primorskaya. Major credit cards accepted. Reception: 356 4135, 356 0263; Service bureau: 356 4563; Fax: 356 0094; Telex: 121616 PRIB SU.*

PETERHOF A Swiss-managed hotelship featuring small but comfortable cabins, a superb restaurant with thematic food festivals and an open-air Skybar. *Moored off Naberezhnaya Makarova, near the Tuchkov Bridge. Major credit cards accepted. For reservations from abroad contact I.C.H. Management, tel: +41 55 275617; Fax: +41 55 273174; Telex: 876371 ICH CH. St. Petersburg tel: 213 6321; Fax: 213 3158.*

MID-RANGE

OKHTINSKAYA A French-Russian joint venture that is clean, quiet, comfortable and quite reasonably priced. Located across the river from the Smolny Cathedral and somewhat inconvenient to public transport, the Okhtinskaya has several restaurants, a large and well-equipped business center and saunas. *Bolsheokhtinsky Prospekt 4. Major credit cards accepted. Reception: 227 4438; Reservations fax: 227 2618; Service bureau: 222 8642; Telex: 621612 GELLER.*

ST. PETERSBURG A medium-priced hotel overlooking the Neva, with the standard assortment of bars and mediocre restaurants typical of former Intourist hotels, and a service bureau that says they can arrange anything. This hotel houses the largest convention facilities in the city and has a small business center as well. *Pirogovskaya Naberezhnaya 5/2. Metro: Ploshchad Lenina. MC, Visa, Eurocard. Tel: 542 9411; Service bureau: 542 9560; Fax: 248 8002.*

PULKOVSKAYA This under-rated Finnish-built hotel is opposite the Great Patriotic War monument on Moskovsky Prospekt on the southern edge of the city (20 minutes by metro to the city center). In the Finnish tradition it is equipped with a sauna and several bars. *Ploshchad Pobedy 1. Metro: Moskovskaya. Major credit cards accepted. Reception: 264 5122; Service bureau: 264 5116.*

MOSKVA Across the street from the picturesque Alexander Nevsky Monastery, the former Intourist-run Hotel Moskva is a fairly typical medium-class Soviet-style hotel. Their smorgasbord (*shvedsky stol*) allows you to consume large quantities of reasonably palatable food, and there is a Neva Star hard currency shop in the lobby. *Ploshchad Alexandra Nevskogo 2. Metro: Ploshchad Alexandra Nevskogo. Reception: 274 2052, 274 2051; Service bureau: 274 2058; Fax: 274 2130.*

KARELIA A modest hotel on the eastern fringe of the city, the Karelia has an excellent reputation for good service. *Ulitsa Marshala Tukhachevskogo 27, korpus 2. Metro: Ploshchad Lenina then trolleys 3, 12 or 19. Major credit cards (except American Express) for accommodation only. Tel: 226 32 38, 226 3026; Fax: 226 3511.*

OKTYABRSKAYA A cheaper, centrally located hotel that has satellite television. It's across from the Moscow Train Station. Did we mention that it was cheap? *Ligovsky Prospekt 10. Metro: Ploshchad Vosstaniya. Tel: 277 6330; Service bureau: 277 6012.*

HELEN Formerly part of the SOVIETSKAYA Hotel, this wing has been taken over by a Finnish-Russian joint venture. *Lermontovsky Prospekt 43/1. Metro: Tekhnologichesky Institut. Tel: 113 0925, 251 6101; Fax: 113 0859; Telex: 121 349 HELEN SU.*

ROSSIYA A classic Soviet-style hotel, good for nostalgia buffs. Almost no English spoken, a "restaurant" serving institutional food and the rooms are not half-bad. Pretty cheap. *Ploshchad Chernyshevskogo 11. Metro: Park Pobedy. Tel: 296 3146; Reservations: 296 7349.*

Coming Soon
THE COMMODORE HOTEL, a refurbished American luxury cruise liner, will arrive in summer 1993 and take up permanent residence in St. Petersburg. The Commodore promises to be a welcome addition to the city providing comfortable waterfront lodgings and fine on-board dining, entertainment and a choice of indoor or outdoor bars all with a distinctly American flare. *Scheduled opening August 1993. For reservations and booking information (Sweden) tel: +46 8 660 0210; Fax: +46 8 662 7670*

BUDGET

Although it seems like an ideal budget destination, Russia on the cheap has never been as accessible as it should be. However, with the old restrictions on foreigners fading away and the growing interest in independent travel, hosteling Russia is emerging to provide a safe, comfortable and relatively cheap alternative to the high priced organized tour circuit.

Hosteling International, with member hostels in **Estonia** and **Finland**, provides visa assistance and ticket reservations for travel to St. Petersburg and the rest of Russia, as well as access to current information about budget travel in this part of the world. *Eurohostel Helsinki Linnankatu 9, SF-00160 Helsinki. Tel: +358 0 66 44 52; Fax: +358 0 65 50 44. Estonian Youth Hostel Liivalaia 2, Tallinn. Tel: +372 2 441096.*

ST. PETERSBURG YOUTH HOSTEL Located in Petersburg's center a 10 minute walk from the Moscow Train Station, the St. Petersburg Youth Hostel has been serving budget travellers since the summer of 1992. As an official member of the Russian Youth Hostel Association and Hosteling International, they can provide assistance for every aspect of a budget trip to Russia from full visa support and reservations to domestic and international train tickets. The rooms are clean with three to five beds in each and special arrangements can be made for couples. You can book from the USA, Helsinki and through Hosteling International offices throughout Europe. They also handle Estonian visa support and hostel reservations in Tallinn. International telephone, fax and E-mail services available. *3rd Sovetskaya 28. Metro: Ploshchad Vosstaniya. Booking well in advance is advisable. To book in the USA contact Russian Youth Hostels, 409 North Pacific Coast Highway, Bldg. #106, Suite 390, Redondo Beach, California, 90277. Tel: +1 (310) 379 4316; Fax: +1 (310) 379 8420. St. Petersburg tel: 277 0569; Fax: 277 5102.*

RITM-CENTURION Located smack in the middle of a mini-Stalinist-constructivist city, this small hotel (8 rooms in all) is pretty cheap with relatively nice rooms. They haven't quite got the hang of Western-style service though, and in order to get into the hotel (keys to the outside door are not given out) you have to try to explain to the *dezhurnaya* who you are and why you expect her to open the door. The restaurant has a "colorful" atmosphere reminiscent of the farmers' markets. *Turbinnaya Ulitsa 11. Metro: Narvskaya. Tel: 186 7689; Fax: 186 0459.*

Sputnik
The youth-travel organization **Sputnik** has proved much more durable than Intourist and has managed to keep its hold on several youth hotels splattered around the city. For the most part these are standard 1-2 star deals with no-nonsense single and double rooms, the majority without bath. All the hotels have some kind of eating facility serving food-like matter. Most are located outside the city center. Where Sputnik stick their clients depends on the price of the tour. Theoretically only Sputnik tour groups can receive lodgings in Sputnik hotels, though a surprising number of tourists and small companies are lodged in the LDM Palace of Youth (listed below). Note that when you book a tour you will be charged a lump sum which includes excursions and some meals and skipping out on these will not result in a refund (but may keep you healthier). Reservations can be made through the Sputnik head office in St. Petersburg or through many foreign travel agencies. *Ulitsa Chapygina 4. Metro: Petrogradskaya. Tel: 234 3500; Fax: 234 2304.*

Some Sputnik Hotels
SPUTNIK Unspectacular and not too un-centrally located, this clean and relatively safe hotel has a small casino and a good hairdresser's downstairs. *Prospekt Morisa Toreza 34. Metro: Ploshchad Muzhestva. Reception tel: 552 5632.*

LDM PALACE OF YOUTH   Filled with roaches and tiny companies, the Palace has a casino and a disco that sometimes has live concerts.   *Ulitsa Professora Popova 47.   Metro: Petrogradskaya.   Tel: 234 3278.*

Alternatives
OLGINO MOTEL CAMPING   Located about 30 minutes northwest of the city on the road to Finland, Olgino is a Soviet-style youth motel and campground.   A favorite hang-out of mafia goons and highwaymen, as well as tourists on their way to and from Finland. *18 kilometers northwest of Petersburg on the Primorskoye Shosse.   Accessible by elektrichka to Olgino station. Reception: 238 3009; Reservations and service bureau: 238 3550.*

APARTMENT RENTALS

Short term rental of private apartments is a concept that has not yet caught on big here, though this should not come as a surprise as the vast majority of people are themselves waiting for an upgrade in their personal accommodations. If you have any Russian friends or business associates, ask them for help. At some train stations (Moskovsky and Varshavsky), old ladies greet trains from major cities by standing around holding signs saying (in Russian) "room for rent" (Сдаю комнату).   As a rule they do not speak English, meaning negotiations and descriptions can be somewhat tricky. Bear in mind that rooms for rent are in **communal apartments**, one of those wonderful socialist inventions thought up in the 1920s by the Minister of Education.   The goal was to break down individual bourgeois family ties and integrate people into one big happy Socialist family sharing the same bathroom and kitchen.   Not surprisingly the experiment flopped; people came to loathe their neighbors and occasionally turned them in to the police.

For those staying **long term**, there are several agencies that handle apartment rentals. Apartment prices vary considerably and rarely do you get what you pay for as people try to extract as much currency as possible based on the premise that they really need the money. As a general rule, apartments in St. Petersburg, especially in the center, are rundown and are full of surprises (exploding sockets, hot water shutdowns, creepy crawlies and sudden rent increases). Keep in mind that in the summer months all central hot water is shut off for four to eight weeks so if your apartment doesn't have its own water heater it's either cold showers or the bucket method.

InterOccidental An American-Russian joint venture that moves large volumes of real estate and also does some rentals. *Ulitsa Vosstaniya 49, suite 25. Metro: Chernyshevskaya. Tel: 273 4323, 272 1857; Fax 272 8031.*

Dinat'f A good selection of somewhat pricey apartments in the city center. *Ligovsky Prospekt 72, apt. 12. Metro: Ligovsky Prospekt. Tel/fax: 112 0765.*

Petropolitana Tours arranges short and long term rentals, as well as visa support and tourist services. *P.O. Box 134, St. Petersburg 194021. Tel: 232 3672; Fax: 532 5473.*

Deon A wide range of apartments from cheapies out in the boondocks to nicer, more central places. *Suvorovsky Prospekt 62. Metro: Ploshchad Vosstaniya then trolley 5 or 7. Tel: 110 7045, 271 2884.*

MOVING AROUND THE CITY

TRANSPORTATION CAN BE divided into two basic groups: public and private. Public transport (the metro and above-ground transport) is dirt cheap, though it is far from user-friendly, usually packed like a can of sardines and it doesn't smell much better. Private transport (taxis and hired cars or buses) are of course more expensive, though prices for the most part can still be considered reasonable by Western standards. As is often the case in this country, there is no middle ground - either you sweat it out with the rank-and-file on the municipal offerings, or you can cruise around in the considerable luxury of your own private machine.

METRO

*"Riding the metro means
never having to say 'I'm sorry'"*.

Orientation
The St. Petersburg Metro operates from 05:30 to 00:30 and unless you really want intimate contact with the Russian people (all of them at once), try to avoid travelling during the peak commuter hours of 08:00 to 10:00 and 16:00 to 18:00. Stations are indicated by a large "M" and as you approach you will see two sets of doors, one for incoming (marked Вход) and one for outgoing (marked Нет входа). It's pretty easy to see which is which - just go with the flow. The doors weigh about ten tons and swing back and forth with the force of a wrecking ball.

Turnstiles are automated and operate with tokens (*zhetony*) which can be purchased from the small windows or booths marked **Продажа жетонов**. Place your token in the slot, wait for it to drop and for the light to change and walk through. Be aware that if you don't pay your fare or if you walk through before your coin drops, the turnstiles will try to smash your legs with automatic gates triggered by electric eyes. Okay, it doesn't really hurt, but it is pretty frightening.

Passes
Monthly passes are sold during the last four or five days of each month, but rarely after the third of the month. Half-monthly passes are sold from around the 14th of each month for people who missed the boat at the month's beginning. Passes are very convenient as they can be used on all city public transport, and if you are staying in town long they're a necessity. You can find them in ticket booths at metro stations, in kiosks near metro stations and sometimes on tables in underpasses throughout the city. There are monthly metro passes and monthly and half-monthly (second half of the month only) passes for all public transport. Both are called *kartochka*, though the pass for all transport is distinguishable by the fact that it is the most expensive and has the word Единый written across it. Sometimes the person selling the pass will sell a display case for it; it's worth picking up one of these too. To use the pass, go to the turnstile nearest the guard booth, show the guard your pass and walk through.

The metro is very deep because it passes through soggy marshland under the canals and rivers. Incredibly long escalators plummet into the earth, so if you're afraid of heights it's a good idea to stand sideways (the escalator ride at Ligovsky Prospekt, the deepest metro station, takes about two minutes). Many of the stations were designed with huge built-in bomb shelters and civil defense classes instructed Leningraders to go to the nearest metro in the event of a nuclear attack. Kids love to slide small coins down the gutter next to the escalator handrails so don't be surprised if these go whizzing past you. The left side of the escalator is a passing lane so keep to the right unless you want to jog. Emergency stop switches are located near the top and bottom of the escalator, labelled СТОП. Turn these to stop the escalator in an emergency, or just to be annoying.

Getting Around on the Metro

The St. Petersburg Metro is not all that difficult to use. There are four color-coded lines crossing the city and it is undoubtedly the most convenient way to get around. There is a definite lack of maps within the metro although they are located at station entrances, before the turnstiles, and there is usually one in each carriage though in big crowds this is of little help. You may have trouble at first because there are few signs indicating which station you are in, and at some of the stations outer doors prevent you from seeing out of the carriage. Pay close attention to the announcements, even if you don't speak Russian, as they follow a definite pattern.* As a train pulls into a station an announcement is made stating the present station first, immediately followed by the words *"Sleduyushchaya stantsiya"* and the name of the next stop. This can be confusing as it can give you the impression that you are one station ahead of where you are. *"Ostorozhno, dvery zakryvayutsya"* means "Caution, doors are closing." Take this pretty literally; doors on the metro close pretty hard.

To change from one line to another, follow the overhead signs that say Переход. To get out, follow the ones that say Выход в город.

Etiquette

Kill or be killed. Sweet looking *babushkas* will elbow you or shove you out of their way. Don't get upset when you are

---

*These recorded announcements are having a difficult time adjusting to the post-Communist era and thus may refer to certain metro stations by their old names. For instance you may hear *Ploshchad Mira* and *Krasnogvardeiskaya* announced instead of *Sennaya Ploshchad* and *Novocherkasskaya*.

pushed, shoved or stepped on - there's just no getting around it and it's nothing personal. In order to negotiate an exit from crowded trains it is standard to ask the person standing between you and the doors if they will get off at the next stop, *"Vy seychas vykhoditye?"* The assumption is that anyone intending to get off at the next stop will have already jockeyed into escape position, so a "yes" answer is license for being latched onto and having stale alcohol breathed down your neck. A "no" answer will result in the inquirer clawing and elbowing past you to get closer to the door until they find someone who is getting off.

It is expected that you will give up your seat to the elderly, the handicapped and people with small children so if one of the above stands in front of you, stand up, point to your seat and mumble *"pazhalsta."* Failure to do this may result in a diatribe about how nobody has any manners anymore while everyone else looks on in relief that the lecture is directed at you and not them.

TRAMS, BUSES AND TROLLEYS

TRAMS, BUSES AND TROLLEYS

Orientation

Above-ground transport operates from 05:20 to around 01:00 (on weekends it stops running earlier) and it shuts down as promptly as the metro, so leave yourself plenty of time. Above-ground transport routes are subject to permanent changes as the number of vehicles gradually diminishes and temporary changes when streets get dug up. Your best bet is to acquire a Municipal Transport Routes Map available at some kiosks and stores that sell maps. Know in advance where you will be getting off as stops throughout the city can be quite far apart and a missed stop can result in a fifteen minute walk.

If you don't have a monthly pass then you will need to purchase tickets (*talony*) to ride on above-ground transport. These are sold in strips of 10 from some kiosks and from most drivers during stops, though sometimes they are out (usually indicated by a small handwritten sign hanging in the driver's box that says Нет талонов). Take one of these tickets and punch it in the little metal boxes that hang by the windows. If you can't reach one, give your ticket to the person between you and the box and he or she will do it for you. It's basically the honor system, though every now and then an inspector will come on board and ask to see people's tickets or passes. If you have nothing to show him you will be issued an on-the-spot fine in rubles, and pleading *no comprendo* rarely works. Sure, these fines are low and many people don't bother to buy tickets, but it can be embarrassing to get caught. Luckily above-ground transport is usually so crowded that inspectors don't bother to get on.

Trams are one of the most picturesque ways of moving around the city (assuming you can squeeze yourself into position near a window) as they generally travel on smaller side streets. They are the slowest of all of St. Petersburg's public transport and the least reliable (when one breaks down it blocks the entire line, often for the rest of the day). Stops are marked by a sign with a Latin "T" on a white rectangular board hanging over the tracks which also states the tram numbers.

Trolleys are electric buses and are recognizable by their arms reaching up to the power lines and the absence of clouds of noxious exhaust. Trolleys are generally the most frequent and usually the most crowded form of public transport (especially along Nevsky). Stops are marked by a large Cyrillic "T" (m) or a blue and white sign stating the line numbers and a red Latin "T" inside a white triangle. Occasionally the electric arms will fall off the power lines, stopping traffic and forcing the driver to run around the back with a large pole and risk electrocution in order to get the trolley running again.

Buses are usually the Hungarian-made *Icarus* that are in use throughout the former Eastern Bloc. They are generally the form of transport that requires the most patience, as spare parts have become both scarce and expensive and lines run less and less frequently. Bus stops are marked by "A" signs (for *avtobus*) at the roadside, with yellow boards listing the line numbers.

There are a number of new **express buses** cruising around the city. These red, coach-type buses are denoted by the Latin letter "T" before the line number (for instance T-10 runs along most of the regular 10 bus route). They are several times more expensive and thus significantly less crowded than regular buses. Monthly passes and *talony* are no good on these; pay the driver as you get off. They will stop more or less anywhere along their route for passengers to get on or off.

Etiquette
The same rules on giving up your seat and negotiating an exit are in force as on the metro. Above-ground transport is definitely something you should experience...once.

TAXIS

Any vehicle can serve as a taxi. Ambulances can be flagged down, as well as trucks, off-duty buses, army jeeps, private cars and, on occasion, official city taxis. Many drivers cruise the streets in order to make a few extra rubles. For the most part these rides are safe and not too expensive, though prices are rising at a spectacular rate. Hail a taxi by sticking your arm out and when a vehicle stops open the door and state your destination. The driver will either tell you to get in, name a price, ask you to offer a price, or say no and drive away. If you don't speak Russian this negotiation can be a little tricky, especially given the fact that the standard price for a ride anywhere for a foreigner is five dollars. But not that tricky...

Learn your numbers... Taxi prices are rounded off to the nearest hundred rubles (see *Language*).

Know your destination... Say it over and over until you say it smoothly before even attempting to hail a cab. Know the neighborhood it's in and the approximate distance from where you are.

Don't renegotiate... The unwritten rules say that a negotiated price can't be changed, so even if the driver does figure out you're foreign (and he will), don't fork over five bucks. Actually, don't fork over five bucks to anyone in this town.

A Word on Prices
Like everything else here, fares are constantly increasing. They are usually posted on the dashboard of official taxis on a little white card filled with confusing text and numbers. The important number is the very last one; this is a multiplier for drivers who use the meter. In other cars you'll just need to make an offer that seems reasonable, or let the driver make one of his own.

Russian speakers can **order a taxi** by calling **312 0022**. They will ask the number from where you are calling, the destination, the last name of the person who wants the cab and when it will be needed. If the answer to the last question is anything except "right now", they will usually tell you to call back when you need it and hang up on you; otherwise, the dispatcher will tell you to wait for her to call you back. It is important to keep the phone line free because if the dispatcher tries to call you back and the line is busy you'll get scratched off the list. Sooner or later (usually within 10 minutes) the dispatcher calls back to tell you when the cab will arrive and its license number. You will be required to pay a fee (posted inside the cab) for the order, plus the fare accumulated from the moment the driver received the order. The reliability of this service varies and invariably it will not work just when you need it most.

Safety Tips
As with many things in Russia there is a bit of a racket in taxis, but some common sense will keep you out of trouble. Think twice before getting into a taxi that has more than one person sitting in it; take a good look at who else is in there before making your decision. Taxis that wait outside restaurants, train stations and other privileged positions have to pay off mafiosi for their space and consequently they charge much higher rates, usually in hard currency. Just walking a hundred meters up or down the street will lower the fare considerably. Almost all taxi-related crimes happen after dark and usually with people they pick up on Nevsky or other areas frequented by the well-to-do. It may not be a bad idea to memorize the car's license plates (assuming it has them) in case something bad happens.

DEALING WITH A CAR

Unless you plan to be in town for a long time, the best advice about driving is not to do it. There are plenty of viable alternatives, and the roads are in such a bad state that they will damage your car's suspension system. However, if you are determined, driving in Petersburg can be accomplished though it will take a while to get good at it.

The Basics: To operate a motor vehicle in St. Petersburg you must have the following documents in the vehicle or on your person at all times:

- Your home driver's license and a notarized translation of it or an international driving permit from your home country with a Russian language insert;

- Your passport and visa (a photocopy won't cut it);

- Your car's registration certificate;

- A customs certificate which says that you will take your car back out of the country (unless you've rented it here).

Speed limits are posted in an irregular and haphazard fashion. They are usually 60km/h (37 mph) in the city and 80 or 100km/h (50 or 65 mph) on highways. Traffic coming from the right has the right-of-way. There is no right-on-red law in St. Petersburg and if you don't know what this is you probably come from a country where you drive on the other side of the road.

St. Petersburg uses international(ish) **road signs** which are usually easy to understand. Major highways, and roads leading to them, are usually marked in both Cyrillic and Latin characters (a sign will say, for example, "ТАЛЛИНН/TALLINN").

Safety
It is illegal to operate a motor vehicle after you have consumed any amount of **alcohol** and this is stringently enforced. A traffic cop who suspects you of having consumed even token

amounts of booze will be hard to convince otherwise and he does have the right to impound your car in the interests of safety.

Safety belt use is mandatory and GAI guys (see below) can use the lack of a seat belt as a reason for pulling you over. In response, most Russian drivers place the belt across their shoulder without buckling it. So *there*.

Gasoline (Benzin)
Filling stations are located all over the city and are open when they have gas. All stations are self service; pay before you pump. Periodic shortages or announcements of impending price increases, usually in increments of 200% or so, lead to mind-numbingly long lines outside filling stations. Although prices are rising, it will be a while before they reach European levels. Most stations offer A-76 and A-92 (93) grade, good for Russian-made cars (though imported models will run all right on the latter), and a select few have A-95 for imported cars. Diesel fuel, which is still extremely cheap, is sold at different filling stations with lines that appear longer because huge trucks and buses wait there but are actually shorter.

Neste, the Finnish oil giant, operates several filling stations that have high grade fuel at Finnish prices (i.e. outrageous) and lower grade at Russian prices (dirt cheap). They also sell oil, windshield wiper fluid and antifreeze. *Moskovsky Prospekt 100; Maly Prospekt 68 (Vasilievsky Island); Avangardnaya Ulitsa 36; Pulkovskoye Shosse 34 (by the airport); Ulitsa Savushkina 36. Hard currency or rubles and major credit cards accepted. Diesel sold at the last three addresses.*

Hazards
Theft: The majority of auto-related criminal activity in St. Petersburg involves part theft or malicious damage rather than the theft of the entire vehicle, but the latter is by no means

unknown. All cars from flashy Mercedes to boxy *Zaporozhets* are targets. Remove any valuables (and anything that might be considered valuable: sunglasses, cigarettes, jackets, radios, krugerrands, etc.) from your car when parking, even if it's only for a few minutes. Also remove your windshield wiper blades - there's a perpetual shortage of them in Russia, and if you forget to remove them, someone else undoubtedly will remember. Try to park your car in a guarded lot or where there are a lot of people around.

Accidents: If you're in an accident you are supposed to stop the car immediately and wait for the GAI guys to come and start taking money from everyone involved, even if you're in the middle of a major intersection. Don't expect the other driver's insurance to pick up your bill, because the chances are he doesn't have any.

The GAI Guys
GAI, the State Automobile Inspectorate, has officers posted all around the city to enforce automobile regulations. They can stop you without probable cause, inspect vehicles and impose on-the-spot fines. That's the good news. The bad news is that GAI officers are horribly underpaid and use their powers to stop motorists and extract fines for real or imagined violations, and foreign cars are their favorite target. The really bad news is that they have the legal right to shoot at your vehicle if you fail to pull over.

GAI officers wear a dark blue uniform with a distinctive silver shield on the left breast, a white belt and carry a lit or striped baton. If an officer points his baton at you, you are to pull over right away. If you speak Russian this is the time to use it; the better your Russian, the better chance you have of negotiating your way out of it without losing your pants.

Car Rental
Many agencies offer cars with or without drivers and prices are comparable to those in other European capitals. Due to the abovementioned hazards we strongly recommend that until you are comfortable with the driving environment here you hire a car with a driver.

Transvelltroikka is a Finnish-Russian joint venture that rents out all kinds of cars both with and without drivers. They can arrange to meet you here or anyplace in Finland and cars can be driven across the Finnish border. *Lermontovsky Prospekt 37. Metro: Tekhnologichesky Institut. Hard currency and rubles, major credit cards accepted. Open 08:30-18:00 Mon-Fri, 09:00-15:00 Sat-Sun. Tel: 113 7253, 113 7228; Fax 114 3803. In Helsinki: Tel: +358 90 3513300, +358 90 796980.*

AVIS offers Peugeots and minibuses and they can arrange to have you met at the airport with a car and driver. *Konnogvardeisky Bulvar 4, entrance 6, room 34. Credit cards only: Visa, MC, EC, no cash or travellers cheques accepted. Open 09:00-18:00 Mon-Sat. Tel: 110 64 96, 311 24 13; Telex: 121732 CGTT SU.*

Avtodom rents cars, limousines and Mercedes buses with drivers. Cheaper than most, but you need to make a reservation by fax or in person at least a day in advance. They have facilities to handle handicapped passengers on their buses. *Naberezhnaya Reki Moiki 56. Metro: Nevsky Prospekt. Hard currency and rubles. Open 10:00-18:00 daily. Tel/fax: 315 9043.*

Interavto, a joint venture with Hertz, rents out Mercedes and Volvo sedans and minibuses. *Perekupnoi Pereulok 4. Metro: Ploshchad Alexandra Nevskogo. Hard currency and rubles. Open 09:00-21:00 daily. Tel: 277 4032, 274 2060 (24 hours).*

A Final Something to Keep in Mind...
Drawbridges that cross the larger rivers rise with a vengeance at different times between 02:00 and 05:00 to let ships pass through when the river isn't frozen solid. Note that although the smaller bridges come down again for a time, the large bridges crossing the Neva River stay up for the entire interval. Plan ahead and remember...up means up.

Hours of Upness

Alexandra Nevskogo Bridge	02:35 - 04:50
Birzhevoi Bridge	02:25 - 03:20 and 03:40 - 04:40
Bolsheokhtinsky Bridge	02:45 - 04:45
Bolshoi Krestovsky Bridge	02:05 - 02:35 and 04:45 - 05:20
Bolshoi Petrovsky Bridge	01:25 - 02:00 and 05:00 - 05:45
Dvortsovy Bridge	01:55 - 03:05 and 03:15 - 04:45
Kamennostrovsky Bridge	02:15 - 03:00 and 04:05 - 04:50
Liteiny Bridge	02:10 - 04:40
Nikolaevsky Bridge	01:55 - 02:55 and 03:15 - 04:50
Sampsonievsky Bridge	02:10 - 02:25 and 03:20 - 04:25
Troitsky Bridge	02:00 - 04:40
Tuchkov Bridge	02:00 - 03:10 and 03:40 -04:40

FOOD AND DRINK

Russian General: "We feed our troops 1,500 calories a day."
American General: "Oh. We feed ours 3,000 calories a day."
Russian General: "But that's impossible! No one can eat two
kilograms of potatoes in one day!"

NOBODY COMES TO RUSSIA for the food. Most people associate the place with long lines and endless variations on the potato theme, though this is a misconception. Russian cuisine, when done right, is actually quite wholesome and dining can be an enjoyable experience. It is also entirely possible to have the same bland and filling meals every day. In either case the visitor will never go hungry; the challenge is to try and make the most out of meals so that they are something to be looked forward to, rather than a nasty way to avoid starvation. Thanks to the economic and political changes of the past few years the restaurant trade has flourished and it has become much easier to fulfill one's gastronomic desires.

Hospitality
Should you be lucky enough to be invited to a Russian home for dinner, be assured that you will get the best of what's on hand and plenty of it. Russians are famed for their hospitality and love to invite people over in order to thoroughly stuff them. It is expected that a guest will accept all that is offered and your host may be offended should you decline. Be prepared for staunch arguments on the part of your host as to why you should eat the lump of raw pork fat or drink the glass of sweet home-made elderberry wine stuck in front of you. These dinners can be one of the most enjoyable aspects of a visit to St. Petersburg and they provide insight into the Russian people and their way of life, especially after the third bottle of vodka.

Note that Russians drink **tea** as though there won't be any available tomorrow, which may not be too far from the truth. In Russia tea is tea - they don't fool around with any of this Earl Grey or Lapsang Souchong nonsense. Some people collect and dry out various leaves during the summertime to brew into their tea, with mint (*myata*) being the most common. Tea is almost never served alone but with some kind of munchies, from little sandwiches to small dishes of home-made jam. Coffee is not quite as prevalent, for which we should all be thankful as it's usually pitifully weak and tastes like it was brewed from fertilizer.

Breakfast can be a beautiful Continental affair with bread, butter, jam, cheeses, sausage, eggs, porridge (*kasha*) and pancakes (*bliny*); it can also be a disappointing way to start the day with a lump of greasy porridge, stale bread and weak over-sweetened tea. It all depends on where you wake up.

Lunch used to be the main meal of the day in Russia, but since the fall of Communism people no longer have the five hours or so of free time in the middle of the day that they used to and so it has become less important than dinner. Lunch begins with a simple appetizer (usually soup and/or salad), followed by a meat or fish dish. To finish, tea or coffee is traditionally served, sometimes with ice cream or pastries.

Dinner, a serious ordeal, begins with appetizers (*zakuski*) which can include smoked fish, cold cuts, caviar, sandwiches and various salads. Next comes the main course, followed by tea or coffee and dessert. Formal dinners at fancy restaurants or at people's homes are events in themselves, with plenty of time in between courses for conversation, copious drinking and dancing.

FOOD AND RELATED TERMS

English	Transliteration	Russian
Breakfast	*Zavtrak*	Завтрак
Lunch	*Obyed**	Обед
Dinner	*Oozhin**	Ужин
First course	*Pervoye blyudo*	Первое блюдо
Appetizers	*Zakuski*	Закуски
Soup	*Sup*	Суп
Salad	*Salat*	Салат
Main Dish	*Vtoroye blyudo*	Второе блюдо
Dessert	*Sladkoye*	Сладкое
Bread	*Khleb*	Хлеб
Rice	*Ris*	Рис
Sausage	*Kolbasa*	Колбаса
Beef	*Myaso*	Мясо
Pork	*Svinina*	Свинина
Lamb	*Baranina*	Баранина
Rabbit	*Krolchatina*	Кролчатина
Chicken	*Kura, kuritsa, tsyplyonok*	Кура, Курица, Цыпленок
Veal	*Telyatina*	Телятина
Ham	*Vetchina*	Ветчина
Dumplings	*Pelmeni*	Пельмени
Fish	*Ryba*	Рыба
Trout	*Forel*	Форель
Sturgeon	*Osetrina*	Осетрина
Herring	*Seld*	Сельдь, Селёдка
Egg	*Yaitso*	Яйцо
Omelette	*Yeeshnitsa*	Яичница
Apple	*Yabloko*	Яблоко
Cucumber	*Ogurets*	Огурец
Tomato	*Pomidor*	Помидор
Potato	*Kartofel*	Картофель
Cabbage	*Kapusta*	Капуста
Sour cream	*Smetana*	Сметана
Milk	*Moloko*	Молоко
Juice	*Sok*	Сок
Tea	*Chai*	Чай
Coffee	*Kofe*	Кофе
Sandwich	*Buterbrod*	Бутерброд

* Note that the word *obyed* is often used to mean the main meal of the day which could be lunch and/or dinner. On holidays, weekends and special occasions a large meal is usually held in the early afternoon, meeting the criteria in content and duration for a dinner but nonetheless known as *obyed*.

SOME RUSSIAN SPECIALITIES

Appetizers and Salads

Ikra (Икра) - Caviar, black (чёрная) or red (красная). Served with eggs, bread and butter, or pancakes. Avoid the deceptive *Belkovaya* (белковая) caviar which looks like black caviar but tastes like soap.

Gryby so smetanoi (Грибы со сметаной) - Mushrooms with sour cream sauce. Served hot or cold and usually quite good.

Stolichny salat (Столичный салат) - The classic Russian salad. The main ingredient is potato; other ingredients depend on what is around that can be hidden by large quantities of mayonnaise.

Vinegrette (Винегрет) - Pickled cabbage, potatoes, beets, carrots and onions are the basis of this salad which, like most other Russian salads, can also include just about anything from meat and fish to very small rocks.

Zalivnoye or Studen (Заливное, Студень) - Cold meat or fish covered with gelatin. Sometimes carrots, peas and floor sweepings can be found in there too. The taste is...well...not for everyone.

Myasnoye or Rybnoye Assorti (Мясное/Рыбное ассорти) - Meat or fish cold cuts. The fishy variation can contain some rather salty aquatic specimens. Quality varies from establishment to establishment.

Salo (Сало) - Thoroughly frightening slabs of pure fat. This Ukranian speciality is probably not the best thing for your arteries.

Soups

Most Russian soups are based on a few key ingredients: beets, cabbage, onions, garlic, carrots, potatoes and stock of meat or bone, and are usually topped with a dollop of sour cream. The naming of soups depends on which ingredient receives the most emphasis or on any strange addition to the usual repertoire. For instance, *borshch* (борщ) is heavy on the beets, whereas *shchi* (щи) favors cabbage. Adding pickles to either *borshch* or *shchi* produces *rassolnik* (рассольник), and adding olives and tomato to *rassolnik* produces *solyanka* (солянка). For ethnic variety, there is the popular *kharcho* (харчо), a thick Georgian soup of meat, onions, tomato, rice and spices.

Meat and Fish Dishes

Shashlyk (Шашлык) - Shishkebab. The piece that looks like solid fat really is.

Kotlety (Котлеты) - Russian hamburgers; the meat is usually cut with breadcrumbs and covered in a semi-sweet reddish sauce that resembles ketchup about as much as these resemble hamburgers.

Escalop (Эскалоп) - Your typical slab of meat - beef, pork or veal.

Kotlety po-Kiyevsky (Котлеты по—киевски) - One of the most famous dishes, Chicken Kiev is a large fried chicken football stuffed with mushrooms and butter. A true expert can cut it in such a way as to squirt hot butter on fellow diners.

Beef Stroganov (Беф Строганов) - In Russia, Beef Stroganov is strips of meat with a thick creamy sauce, just like the TV dinners only better because it was invented here.

Tsyplyonok tabaka (Цыплёнок табака) - Fried Chicken, often quite peppery.

Desserts

Tvorog (Творог) resembles cottage cheese and comes in various degrees of sweetness. Often it is served with sour cream or jam.

Blini (Блины), Russian pancakes, are a common dessert (though they sometimes double as an appetizer or as breakfast) and are often served with *tvorog*, sour cream or jam.

Pirog (Пирог) - This can be a small pastry or a larger cake. Pastries are usually filled with apples, *tvorog*, jam or cabbage.

Tort (Торт) - Russian cakes. Lots of creamy frosting and usually extremely sweet.

Morozhenoye (Мороженое) - Ice cream. Eaten with a vengeance both in cafes and on the street, regardless of the weather. On the street or in simpler establishments there are usually almost two flavors...call it one.

Alcoholic Beverages

In addition to the traditional alcoholic beverages listed below there has been a deluge of alcoholic imports from just about everywhere. In kiosks, bars and restaurants it is now possible to buy Polish blue liqueur, Amaretto from Virginia and, of course, some of that world-famous Romanian red wine. In kiosks the cheapest options are usually various vodkas and grain spirits (96% alcohol). Keep in mind that **to buy Russian vodka from a kiosk is to take your life into your own hands**. A lot of the stuff sold as vodka is really watered-down spirit of mysterious origins (industrial alcohol, floor cleaner and rocket fuel not excluded). A bottle of bad vodka can kill you. It is better to spend a little extra and buy your alcohol at a hard currency or reliable ruble store, or in a bar. The same warning goes for **cognac**, which may be little more than methanol and tea.

Most locally produced vodka, cognac and port wine comes in bottles with non-resealable aluminum tops. Once a bottle is opened it is meant to be finished, and usually is with amazing rapidity.

Standard Drinks

Beer (*Pivo* | Пиво) - There are many arguments about Russian beer amongst foreign visitors to St. Petersburg. Some say it is absolutely horrible, others prefer the epithets "vile and nasty," and still others would rather drink laundry detergent mixed with wee-wee. However, in reality there are some brands that are quite good, though the quality of any one brand is rarely consistent. Be aware that Russian beer is not pasteurized and thus after about four days colonies of tiny hops-based life forms spontaneously generate inside the bottle. The date on the label is the date of production, not the use-by date. These brands are a cut above the rest; *Nevskoye* (Невское), *Baltika* (Балтика), *Prazdnichnoye* (Праздничное), *Tverskoye* (Тверское), *Martovskoye* (Мартовское) and *Petrovskoye* (Петровское).

Champagne (*Shampanskoye* | Шампанское) - In almost every bar, kiosk and restaurant you can find *Sovetskoye Shampanskoye*. It comes in five varieties: brut (брют), which is the driest though varies in quality from bottle to bottle; dry (сухое), which is for some reason more consistent; half-dry (полусухое), which is quite sweet by Western standards; half-sweet (полусладкое), which is like bubbly syrup; and sweet (сладкое), which is as close as one can come to a glucose tolerance test outside a clinic. Ever since sugar became expensive the availability of the sweeter champagnes has dropped dramatically. *Sovetskoye Shampanskoye* may not be *Dom Perignon* but at its cost and rate of consumption you will hardly notice.

Vodka (Водка) - Bearing in mind the above warning about lethal kiosk vodka, when you find a good bottle you will find the quality to be quite high. Preferred brands are *Stolichnaya* (Столичная), *Sibirskaya* (Сибирская), the newer *Pyotr Veliky* (Пётр Великий) and the nearly impossible to find *Golden Ring* (Золотое кольцо). Also drinkable are *Moskovskaya* (Московская), *Russkaya* (Русская) and the unpronounceable *Pshenichnaya* (Пшеничная). As an alternative there are a variety of imports ranging from little-known cheapies, like the picturesque Rasputin from Germany and New Yorkskaya from guess where, to better known brands such as Smirnoff and Finlandia.

Cognac (Коньяк) - Quite a large range of cognac is available, most of it not very good. Armenian (Армянский) is considered the best (except for a brand called *Ararat* which is nasty) and there are Moldavian (Молдавский) cognacs which are quite good and consequently almost impossible to find. Georgian (Грузинский) and Azerbaijani (Азербайжанский) cognacs tend to be inferior. Note that where in the West cognac is enjoyed a glass at a time and a bottle may last for years, here a bottle is lucky if it lasts half an hour.

Wine (Vino | Вино) - This is not a country known for its vintners. Though many wines proudly display award medals, closer examination reveals that these were awarded in competitions that took place in former Socialist countries and republics (Bulgaria, Czechoslovakia, Turkmenistan, etc.) and probably reflect a fear of tank invasions more than actual quality. Wines tend to be sweet, some of them (particularly the Armenian and Azerbaijani variants) sickeningly so. Of stuff made in the former Soviet Union, the best comes from Georgia, Moldavia and the Crimea, which is known for its dessert wines. For red, the extremely rare export-quality Moldavian cabernet is the best, though other Moldavian and Georgian reds are drinkable. Good whites are harder to find, but some Moldavian and Crimean varieties are passable. In addition, wines from former Eastern Bloc countries are becoming more available as well as some French. For a taste of the exotic, try some port (портвейн), which is good for...well...not very much, really. The word марочное on the upper label means the wine is aged, and below this word is another word that feebly tries to cover up the fact that the wine was made last Tuesday.

Spirit (Спирт) - This dangerous concoction has become quite a popular item in recent times for its simple and brutal effectiveness. With 96% alcohol, it can also be used in Molotov Cocktails or as lighter fluid. As with vodka, some of the stuff sold in kiosks as spirit is in fact something else, usually something which will affect your stomach like a glass of sulfuric acid. Home-made spirit, or *samogon*, can be amazingly smooth, amazingly deadly or both, depending on the expertise of the maker. Georgian *samogon* called *chacha* is more flavorful but has the same burn as spirit. All are useful for those who want to know what a frontal lobotomy feels like.

Street Food and Snacks
Street food is a Russian institution. Ice cream, cakes and sweets are readily available from street vendors and some-times things that get passed off as pizzas or pastries can be found. Eat anything with meat in it at your own risk; in a country where meat is either scarce or expensive it should strike you as odd that right here on the street someone is selling cheap meat-filled pastries. There are also countless little cafe-like places for a cup of dark tepid liquid and maybe something to eat. These places tend to be named according to what they serve and as a general rule they are for people seeking to overcome hunger pains without worrying much about taste, or for those looking to get tanked.

Thematic Eateries

Blinnaya (Блинная) - Serves pancakes with a variety of toppings.

Pirozhkovaya (Пирожковая) - Serves pastries (*pirozhki*) stuffed with meat, cabbage, carrots, potatoes and anything else they get their hands on. Note that *pirozhki* come fried or baked; we recommend avoiding the fried ones as the oil is changed about once every Five-Year Plan.

Pyshechnaya (Пышечная) - Serves doughnuts (пышки) in their most basic form - lumps of dough fried in oil and covered in sugar.

Morozhenoye (Мороженое) - Ice cream parlors serving you-know-what, sometimes covered with chocolate sprinkles or sweet colored syrup.

Grill-bar (Гриль-Бар) - The original concept behind grill-bars was to serve grilled chicken. In reality they are just like any other eatery and have unpredictable menus ranging from salads, hot meat dishes and drinks to absolutely nothing.

Shashlichnaya (Шашличная) - Lovers of kebab would be better off seeking it in a cafe or restaurant. The *shashlichnayas* around town are dirty havens for people seeking something to accompany their vodka and beer. Out of town, however, small outdoor *shashlichnayas* are often quite good.

Ryumochnaya (Рюмочная) - Also known as *Razlivochnaya*, these are working-class bars that people dip into for a quick ten shots of vodka on their stagger to or from work.

For a Quick Snack

Baskin Robbins American ice cream for rubles. They don't have 31 flavors but they usually have quite a few. *Nevsky Prospekt 79. Metro: Mayakovskaya. Also Park Lenina 4. Metro: Gorkovskaya. Open 10:00 - 22:00 (though the one at Park Lenina usually stays open much later).*

Grill Diez sells delicious roast chickens of varying degrees of plumpness. They prepare the chickens with a healthy amount of black pepper on the skin and roast them in huge, German-made spit roasters. Take out only. *Kamennostrovsky Prospekt 16. Metro: Gorkovskaya. Open 10:00-21:00 or until they run out of chickens. Tel: 232 4255.*

Polar Fast Food A Finnish-Russian joint venture serving snacks and drinks for hard currency and rubles. They have a cafe near the Hotel Pulkovskaya and three kiosks: in Ploshchad Iskusstv and St. Isaac's Square for currency and by the Elektrosila Metro for rubles. *Cafe address: Moskovsky Prospekt 220. Metro: Moskovskaya. Open 10:00-20:00.*

Bristol Dark, neo-futuristic atmosphere. Funky bubbly non-alcoholic drinks, "pizza", microwaved snacks and German beer on tap for rubles. Occasionally they have *khachapuri*, a Georgian melted-cheese and flatbread snack. *Nevsky Prospekt 22 (down the steps). Metro: Nevsky Prospekt. Open 11:00-20:00.*

Bistro Quick cheap grindage in the center of town. *Ulitsa Gogolya 12. Metro: Nevsky Prospekt. Open 14:00-23:00 Mon-Fri, 12:00-21:00 Sat-Sun.*

Cafe Morozhenoye The oldest ice cream cafe in the city still has traces of its original 1952 interior decor. *Nevsky Prospekt 24. Metro: Nevksy Prospekt. Open 10:00-21:00 (14:00-15:00).*

Iveria Cheap Georgian-esque food. *Ulitsa Marata 35. Metro: Vladimirskaya. Open 12:00-22:00 (17:00-18:00). Tel: 164 7478.*

Catering
Ivan & Co, a Swedish-Russian joint venture, can cover a variety of catering needs from casual breakfasts and brunches to banquets in imperial palaces or on cruise ships. They can also prepare box lunches for people on the go, and they offer a special "rent a Swedish chef" service. *Tel: 294 0252; Fax: 298 1306.*

CAFES AND RESTAURANTS

We have included noteworthy cafes and restaurants which offer good food and a high level of service. This is by no means a complete list as new places open and old places close at a startling rate, and the atmosphere of a cafe or restaurant can also change quite drastically in a short period of time. Any type of star-rating system is more or less pointless and a selection is best made on a restaurant's appearance, its clientele and the advice of others.

As a general rule it is best to make reservations whenever possible as it can be frustrating trying to find a place that has room on the spur-of-the-moment. With Russian-run places this can be somewhat difficult for non-Russian speakers, and a visit to the restaurant or cafe is necessary. Sometimes there may be a sign on the door of a restaurant which reads Извините, у нас мероприятие. This roughly translates as "someone paid us lots of money to hang this sign up and keep you from coming in here, so there" and means that you will need to try some another place.

Unless otherwise specified, the following establishments all take rubles. Many places list their prices in dollars and would prefer to be paid in hard currency but are obliged by law to accept rubles at an arbitrary exchange rate. In response to this several establishments put such a miserable rate on the ruble that it can be cheaper to pay in hard currency. Very few places take credit cards; those that do are noted.

Dinner Shows
Many restaurants have some form of "entertainment". In its milder forms, entertainment consists of a piano-player or other solo musician and provides a mellow mealtime atmo-

sphere. Other establishments place more emphasis on the entertainment, providing outrageous variety shows with chorus-line girls, gypsy dancers, magic acts and live music cranked to such a volume that any conversation will need to be in sign language. These full-blown shows can actually be quite a blast and may well be worth experiencing, if only just to see one of the stranger ways wealthier people enjoy themselves here.

Fine Dining

THE IMPERIAL RESTAURANT, overlooking Nevsky Prospekt from the first floor of the Nevskij Palace Hotel, offers superb continental and exquisitely prepared Russian cuisine. Light entertainment in the evening, and a lavish buffet breakfast is offered every morning. *Nevsky Prospekt 57. Metro: Mayakovskaya. Breakfast 07:00-10:00; Lunch or Sunday brunch 12:00-15:00; Dinner 19:00-23:00. Hard currency, major credit cards accepted. Tel: 275 2001.*

APHRODITE Seafood lovers need look no further than this pleasant European-style restaurant which serves the best sea-denizens in St. Petersburg. Central location, attentive service and a comprehensive menu and wine list make this one of St. Petersburg's premier restaurants. *Nevsky Prospekt 86. Metro: Mayakovskaya. Open 12:00-24:00. Hard currency, major credit cards accepted. Tel: 275 7620.*

RESTAURANT PICCOLO Located in the Hotel Olympia, Piccolo has both European cuisine and Russian specialities. The restaurant has a sea view and live entertainment in the evenings. *Ploshchad Morskoi Slavy. Breakfast 07:30-10:00 Mon-Fri, 08:00-10:30 Sat-Sun; Lunch/dinner 12:00-23:00 daily. Hard currency, major credit cards accepted. Tel: 119 6800.*

THE SWEDISH CONNECTION, located on the first floor of the Nevskij Palace Hotel, is decorated in a maritime theme. A Scandinavian smorgasbord with imported beverages makes it ideal for a quick meal or business lunch. *Nevsky Prospekt 57. Metro: Mayakovskaya. Open 11:00-23:00. Hard currency, major credit cards accepted. Tel: 275 2001.*

THE EUROPE RESTAURANT The Grand Hotel Europe's main restaurant offers five-star dining in a spectacularly restored *art nouveau* setting. Excellent food and service, and they have a decadent Sunday brunch with live jazz music. Look up and gawk at the original stained glass ceiling, look down and gasp at the bill. *Mikhailovskaya Ulitsa 1/7. Metro: Nevsky Prospekt. Breakfast 07:00-10:00; Dinner 18:00-23:00 Mon-Sat. Sunday brunch 12:00-15:00. Hard currency, major credit cards accepted. Tel: 113 8071, 113 8066, extension 6330.*

BELLE LEONE If space aliens materialized in this restaurant they would never know they were in Russia - it's clean, cheery and comfortable, the service excellent and the food (European and Russian cuisine) fantastic. There is a guarded parking lot out front. *Vladimirsky Prospekt 9. Metro: Vladimirskaya or Dostoevskaya. Open 12:00-24:00, in summer until 02:00. Hard currency or rubles. Tel: 113 1670.*

THE BRASSERIE A relaxed and elegant European restaurant in the Grand Hotel Europe. *Mikhailovskaya Ulitsa 1/7. Metro: Nevsky Prospekt. Open 11:00-23:00 Mon-Fri, 15:00-23:00 Sun. Hard currency, major credit cards accepted. Tel: 113 8066, 312 0072.*

Mid-range

DADDY'S STEAK HOUSE is one of Petersburg's most popular restaurants, and for good reason. In addition to well-prepared, sizeable slabs of beef, Daddy's offers fish and pasta dishes and a well-stocked Western-style salad bar. Also a large selection of imported wines, liquors and beers. *Moskovsky Prospekt 73. Metro: Frunzenskaya. Open 11:00-24:00. Hard currency, major credit cards accepted. Tel: 252 7744.*

LE CAFE This chic and centrally located German-Russian joint venture cafe overlooking Nevsky Prospekt offers reasonably priced European and Russian specialties, including a fully-stocked salad bar. Every night they have live music, the non-imposing kind you can eat to. The complex includes a bar with German beer on tap, a room for private parties and a stand-up bistro for rubles. *Nevsky Prospekt 142. Metro: Ploshchad Vosstaniya. Hard currency restaurant and bar open 12:00-02:00, ruble section open 11:00-21:00. Tel: 271 2811.*

PIZZA HOUSE You don't have to come here to enjoy the best pizza in St. Petersburg as Pizza House has a fast and friendly delivery service. They offer nine varieties of pizza made from imported ingredients, as well as grilled dishes, some Italian fare and an extensive imported and domestic wine list. All this and a quiet, unimposing setting make Pizza House a great place to get away from the hurly-burly of Petersburg and relax in comfortable surroundings. *Podolskaya Ulitsa 23. Metro: Tekhnologichesky Institut. Open 11:00-24:00. Hard currency, major credit cards and travellers cheques accepted. Tel: 292 2666.*

PIROSMANI Well-prepared Georgian cuisine in an otherworldly interior. Ask for the table on the island. The acid-trip wall is based on the work of the Georgian artist Pirosmani. For rubles, though rather pricey. *Bolshoi Prospekt 14. Metro: Petrogradskaya then trolleys 1, 7, 9, 12 or 46 down Bolshoi Prospekt. Open 12:00-23:00. Tel: 235 6456.*

IMPERIAL Good Russian food and excellent service in an elegant and unimposing atmosphere. In the evening reservations are a must. Can get pricey in rubles, and they will do their best to make you pay in hard currency. *Kamennostrovsky Prospekt 53. Metro: Petrogradskaya. Open from "around" 13:00 until 24:00. Tel: 234 3296, 234 1742.*

SADKO'S *The* hep place to be in St. Petersburg. Russian yuppies, foreign students and business-types come here to unwind or choose from a menu that changes daily. *Mikhailovskaya Ulitsa 1/7. Metro: Nevsky Prospekt. Open 12:00-24:00. Hard currency only, major credit cards accepted. Tel: 312 0072, 113 8066, ext. 6390.*

ASSEMBLY This ruble restaurant has palatable food and is noteworthy mainly because it is open 24 hours and is centrally located. *Ulitsa Bolshaya Konnyushennaya 9. Metro: Nevsky Prospekt. Open 24 hours. Tel: 314 1537.*

Restaurants with Variety Shows

CAN-CAN For a substantial entrance fee you can enjoy a rather eclectic show and the fixed menu which includes a plethora of high quality appetizers, well-prepared main courses and an extensive wine list. Alternatively you can pay just to get in and order à la carte. There is also a bar next to the restaurant that stays open until the wee hours with some food and entertainment of its own. *Izmailovsky Prospekt 7. Metro: Baltiisky Vokzal or Technologichesky Institut. Open 11:00-17:00 for lunch, 19:00-last guest. The show starts at 21:00. Hard currency only. Reservations a good idea. Tel: 251 7027.*

VOSTOK-ORIENT Located on Krestovsky Island, this Indian-Azerbaijani joint venture has two restaurants - a quiet and comfortable Indian restaurant downstairs and Azeri cooking for rubles upstairs in a huge tiered hall. The variety show (in the upstairs section) includes gypsy dancers, a dance band, a guitar player and other typical variety show acts, and people eat, drink and dance until morning. Excellent food and attentive service. *Primorsky Park Pobedy. No near metro, though trams 21, 33 and 34 go close by. The lower restaurant is open from 12:00-24:00, rubles during the day, hard currency at night. Major credit cards accepted. Upstairs open 21:00-04:00. There is a cover charge to get into the upstairs restaurant. Tel: 235 4618, 235 2804.*

IZMAILOV Finely prepared Russian cuisine. The à la carte lunch is moderately priced; dinner has a fixed menu for a set entry fee, which includes the show - either a gypsy troupe or an excellent folklore group featuring traditional knee-bent Russian dances. *Ulitsa 6th Krasnoarmeiskaya 22. Metro: Baltiisky Vokzal. Open 13:00-16:00, 20:00-until the last guests crawl out. Hard currency only. Tel: 292 6838.*

VENICE This Italian restaurant features a ruble pizzeria and a separate hard currency section with a rather unspectacular show. Pizzas are pretty good and reasonably priced and you can order to take out. *Ulitsa Korablestroitelei 21. Metro: Primorskaya. Open 12:30-23:30 (ruble pizzeria until 23:00). Major credit cards accepted. Tel: 352 1432.*

ARAGVI Georgian food. This place bills itself as an "entertainment center" which includes a variety show, a casino, striptease and billiards. Not too expensive, but the late-night crowd can be pretty rough. *Ulitsa Tukhachevskogo 41. Metro: Finlandsky Vokzal then trolley 3, 12 or 19. Open 12:00-06:00 (19:00-20:00). Tel: 225 0804.*

Cafes

KOREAN HOUSE This small, cozy cafe serves good food at reasonable prices. Simple Korean dishes from kim che and spicy carrots to hot noodle soup and marinated beef. *Naberezhnaya Reki Fontanka 20. Metro: Gostiny Dvor. Open 12:00-21:00. Best to make reservations for dinner. Tel: 275 7203.*

SIRIN is a reasonably priced cafe serving classic Russian food and a lots of drinks in a comfortable environment. There are phones at each of the tables, ideal for business lunches or for calling the guys at the next table and telling them to shaddup. *1st Liniya 16, Vasilievsky Island. Metro: Vasileostrovskaya and a 15 minute walk. Open 11:00-24:00. Tel: 213 7282.*

CAFE Aptly named and tucked away under an archway across from the Engineer's Castle, this small hip eatery has good food and a large selection of vodka and beer. It is pretty popular and they don't take reservations, but they stay open real late. *Naberezhnaya Reki Fontanka 14. Metro: Chernyshevskaya and a 15 minute walk to the river. Open 14:00-05:00 (22:00-23:00).*

LITERATURNOYE CAFE Pretty good food and stone-faced service in a pleasant atmosphere with classical music (piano and/or rotund opera-singing types) in the evening. To make a reservation you need to go there and buy a ticket, otherwise just show up and hope they have room. *Nevsky Prospekt 18. Metro: Nevsky Prospekt. Open 12:00-17:00 and 19:00-23:00. Tel: 312 8536.*

CAFE 01 This small cafe is ultra-popular with the Russian business crowd and it can be hard to get in. Well prepared Russian food at reasonable prices and a variety of drinks including some imported beer on tap, all served by long-legged waitresses in short skirts. *Karavannaya Ulitsa 5. Metro: Gostiny Dvor. Open 12:00-23:00 (16:00-16:45). To make a reservation you need to go there and leave some money as hostage.*

TETE A TETE A more refined cafe-restaurant that has small tables seating two and four. In the evening a piano player provides light entertainment. The food is pretty good and the service attentive. Great place to take a date. Evening dress required for dinner - men without ties will not be admitted. *Bolshoi Prospekt 65 (Petrogradskaya Storona). Metro: Petrogradskaya. Open 13:00-23:30. Reservations a must (call between 12:00-13:00), and they require that you go and pick up an invitation card in advance. Tel: 232 7548.*

KROONK Medium priced, well-prepared Armenian cuisine in a nice quiet setting. *Solyanoy Pereulok 14. Metro: Chernyshevskaya. Open 12:00-21:00. Tel: 273 1691.*

EVROPA Another trendy little cafe popular with the same types that frequent Cafe 01. Good Russian fare; make reservations (in Russian) because this place is small. *Ulitsa Soyuza Pechatnikov 19, near the Mariinsky Theater. Open 12:00-23:00. Tel: 113 6072.*

CAT This small freshly-opened cafe belongs to a newly emerging class of Russian eating establishments (Cafe 01 and Evropa belong to this class as well) - hipsters, bandits, businessmen, good food and expensive drinks. *Stremyannaya Ulitsa 22. Metro: Mayakovskaya. Open 13:00-24:00 (16:00-17:00). Tel: 311 3377.*

TBILISI The first co-operative to open in St. Petersburg, this Georgian cafe suffers from inconsistency; sometimes the food is fantastic, other times it is barely passable. The service is always good. *Sytninskaya Ulitsa 10. Metro: Gorkovskaya. Open 12:00-23:30. Drinks for hard currency. Tel: 232 7548.*

BAGHDAD CAFE Lots of good cheap Azerbaijani food. This place is popular, particularly amongst the younger workers of the consulates located nearby and it can be hard to get seats. *Furshtadtskaya Ulitsa 35. Metro: Chernyshevskaya. Open 12:00-23:00. Tel: 272 2355.*

THINGS TO SEE AND DO

S T. PETERSBURG IS A CITY with something for everyone. It is possible to wade through the seeping culture of museums, cruise the grey netherlands of socialist monolithic suburbia, witness history in the making and still make it back in time for supper. Evenings can be spent taking in a concert or ballet, dancing to the latest grooves with yups and hipsters, or delving into the ever-expanding St. Petersburg bar scene. The city has so much to offer that it is virtually impossible to do everything.

There's no need to be frightened into hiding in hard currency establishments and museum tour groups. It is well worth taking some time to look deep into the soul of St. Petersburg. Wander the back streets and canal embankments, peer into the courtyards, stairwells and shops, have a locally brewed beer in front of a metro station and ride a trolley during rush hour. Time spent outside the sanctity of your hotel, air-conditioned or heated bus and insulated tour group is time spent in the real St. Petersburg. Tour organizers assume they are doing you a favor by shielding you from local realities, but give it a try anyway; it can only add to your understanding of the complexities of this place.

MUSEUMS

The city center is packed full of architectural and cultural wonders with enough palaces, museums and sights to overwhelm even the hungriest of culture-vultures. The Hermitage, of course, is the *créme de la créme*, *pièce de résistance* and the *huevos rancheros* of Petersburg's museum scene as well as the largest tourist attraction in the city, and there are plenty of other museums covering a wide variety of topics and interests. Unfortunately, several lesser-known museums are closing, some due to lack of interest and funding (like the Communications Museum), others (such as the Central Lenin Museum and the History of the Young Communist League Museum) for ideological reasons. And for all those agrogeologists out there, we regret to announce that the Soil Science Museum is closed for repairs, and in response to our inquiry as to a proposed re-opening date they laughed before hanging up on us. Although it is extremely unlikely that any of the major museums will close in the near future, the fate of the more eclectic museums in the following list is unforeseeable as government funding is in sharp decline. So don't be heartbroken if you don't get to see the Arctic Exploration exhibition - we're close enough to the Arctic that it wouldn't be all that hard to just go and explore it yourself.

Almost all museum exhibits are described in Russian although for tidy sums of hard currency major museums provide guided tours in English and other languages. These tours occur at certain times of the day, and you usually need to make an advance reservation (though for an extra handful of cash the museum authorities will no doubt be able to arrange a spontaneous tour). As an alternative, many tourist agencies and hotel service bureaus can arrange museum tours for non-Russian speakers. Some museums sell books in English but as these vary in quality (not to mention availability) they shouldn't be relied upon to get the most out of a museum or sight. Except of course for the book you have in your hands, which is gospel.

Most museums and other tourist attractions have higher admission prices for foreigners. While some may be irked by this kind of discrimination, keep in mind that the higher prices for those who can afford it help to support these organizations now that government funding is in decline, and lower prices for locals keep St. Petersburg's cultural heritage affordable and accessible. All right, all right, we hate it too. Since the introduction of such pricing policies, ticket-taking *babushkas* at the exhibition entrances have developed a skilled eye at picking out foreigners (by their clothes, their walk, the presence of large pieces of modern photo equipment and so on), so having a native Russian buy you a ticket is unlikely to help you beat the system. The most popular and therefore most expensive museums have currency exchange booths located on the premises to ensure that people who didn't bring enough rubles can get some more at an absolutely odious rate.

Any bags larger than a ladies' handbag must be checked at the cloakroom. They are very strict about this rule because stealing from museums is a privilege accorded only to the museum administration. If you are planning on photographing or videotaping while inside the exhibition you must pay a flat fee at the ticket office and they will give you a little photo permit. Show this permit to the nice *babushka* who takes tickets and she will not try to break your camera. The *babushka* is completely immune to innocent pleas of "I promise I won't photograph anything" or philosophical inquiries into the definition of handbag. If you are worried about checking anything of great value, then don't bring it to the museum in the first place. You also must check your coat, no matter how cold it is in the museum; any attempt to enter the exhibition area in your coat will result in a barrage of squawking and finger-pointing which is quite embarrassing. Some museums with fancy wooden floors make you attach large strange slipper-like devices to your shoes, gargantuan *tapochki* of sorts. These greatly facilitate sliding around from exhibit to exhibit and are one of the highlights of a visit to a Russian museum, but are a death-trap for anyone wearing high heels.

The story of the **Hermitage collection** begins with Catherine II. Soon after assuming the throne, Catherine decided that in the tradition of cultured, enlightened empresses she would gather an art collection. She knew practically nothing about art but she had a lot of money to spend, and in 1764 she made her first acquisition - 225 Dutch and Flemish paintings bought from the Berlin merchant Gotskowsky, who needed to pay off some debts. This acquisition marked the beginning of Catherine's "painting fever" where she embarked on a mission to build up as large a collection as fast as she could.

Russian Ambassadors in Europe were given the extra task of taking part in art auctions and buying as much as possible. Catherine also received assistance from some of her famous correspondents, including Diderot and Voltaire. Whole collections were swooped up with Imperial money, including not only paintings but sketchings, carvings, applied arts, medals, money and books (including Voltaire's library). As the collection rapidly expanded, a second building (The Small Hermitage) was built to house the overflow in 1775, and a third soon followed in 1787 (The Old Hermitage).

After Catherine's death, subsequent emperors continued to enlarge the collection, though not at her insane pace. In 1814 Alexander I, fresh from his victory over Napoleon, bought the private collection of Napoleon's wife Josephine at a tremendous discount .

After the 1917 Revolution the collection swelled when the private collections of the city's wealthiest families - the Yusupovskys, Stroganovs, Sheremetovs and Shuvalovs - were "annexed" along with the finest items from the imperial palaces at Peterhof and Gatchina. The only time the collection ever shrank war during Stalin's reign when a few paintings (among them some Rembrandts and Rubens) and Fabergé eggs were sold in the West. In 1964 The Hermitage was awarded the Order of Lenin by the Presidium of the Supreme Soviet (bet you won't hear much about *that* anymore).

THE HERMITAGE

The largest museum collection in the world is spread throughout four buildings. The main entrance is located in the **Winter Palace**; the next building to the east is the **Little Hermitage**; further east lies the **Old Hermitage** (facing the river) and the **New Hermitage** (facing Palace Square). An arched gallery spans the Winter Canal and leads to the **Hermitage Theater**.

Each of the four buildings is an architectural gem both inside and out, with regal façades, opulent staircases, frescoes, gold, statues and interesting theme rooms. The art collection spans pre-history to the late 20th century with impressive collections of Matisse, Rembrandt, Goya, Degas, Gaugain, Picasso and a zillion others. There is usually at least one temporary exhibition someplace in the Hermitage; a sign on the ground floor near the ticket booth lists these. Also worth seeing is the **Treasury Collection** on the ground floor of the Old Hermitage, accessible only by booking in advance at the ticket booth. The Hermitage Theater can be reached by a passageway from the northeast corner of the Old Hermitage but is usually only open to guided tour groups.

It is impossible to see the entire collection in one visit, so don't wig out on the first day. Existing maps and guides can be confusing because doors get opened and shut and exhibits moved, meaning that you must negotiate a maze of galleries and staircases before finding your beloved *oeuvre*. The surest way to find any specific artist is to ask one of the *babushkas* who sit and watch the individual rooms. They don't speak English, but saying the name of the artist will be sufficient to have her point you in the right direction. Note that on weekends the crowds can be pretty incredible, especially in the afternoon and in the summer.

Dvortsovaya Naberezhnaya 34, entrance from the Neva Embankment. Metro: Nevsky Prospekt then trolleys 1, 7 or 10 to Dvortsovaya Ploshchad or 15 minute walk. Open 10:30-18:00 daily except Mon, 10:30-17:00 Sun. Recorded information in Russian: 219 8625; Excursion bureau: 219 8727.

THE RUSSIAN MUSEUM

After the Hermitage, the Russian Museum is definitely #2, although this is a bit like comparing Beethoven to Barry Manilow. The museum is located in the former Mikhailovsky Palace, behind the gesticulating Pushkin in *Ploshchad Iskusstv*. Built for Paul I's youngest son, the palace was made into a museum by Nicholas II in 1898. The Russian Museum is perhaps the most frustrating museum in the city, not for reasons of crowds (which can be quite heavy on weekends and during school holidays) but because they keep most of the really interesting stuff (such as Kandinsky, Malevich and Filonov) either locked in the basement or on tour around the world and the display is over-ladened with the boring stuff (Realism).

On the *Kanal Griboyedova* side of the museum, just down the street from the Church of the Bleeding Savior, is the entrance to the **Benoir Wing,** where they hold special exhibitions which are often more interesting than the permanent exhibits. Behind the museum are the spacious Mikhailovsky Gardens.

Inzhenernaya Ulitsa 4. Metro: Nevsky Prospekt. Open 10:00-18:00 daily except Tues. Tel: 314 3448.

PETER AND PAUL FORTRESS

Designed to protect newly acquired lands from invading Swedes (it worked - the Swedes were kept at bay for almost three centuries and only now are able to realize their historic imperial ambitions through trendy restaurants and luxury hotels), the hexagonal shaped Peter and Paul Fortress lost its military significance before it was completed. Its guns never saw any action and were put to use as a flood warning signal, and the fortress housed a political prison for 200 years. One of its first prisoners was Alexis, Peter the Great's own son, accused of subversion and treason and subsequently tortured to death under Peter's supervision. Other famous prisoners interned here were the Decembrists (five hanged, over one hundred packed off to Siberia), Dostoevsky (subjected to a mock execution and exiled to Siberia), Lenin's brother (hanged) and the writer of revolutionary leaflets, Maxim Gorky (vilified as a hero of the Socialist cause).

The **St. Peter and Paul Cathedral** is the sacred burial place of every Russian tsar since Peter and contains some bodacious icons. The **Engineer's House** is now an architecture museum with an exhibition showing how the city was built, and the **Trubetskoi Bastion**, the former interrogation center, is also open for viewing. Also within the complex is the **Mint**, built in the beginning of the 19th century. Slightly off-the-wall is the **Museum of Gas-Dynamic Laboratories** in the Iohann Wing featuring an exhibition of spacemen paraphernalia and other bizarre things whose connection to the concept of this fortress are somewhat obscure. In the gardens there is an interesting and controversial monument by local artist Shemiakin to Peter the Great. Unveiled in May, 1991, the monument stirred controversy because it portrays Peter not as a majestic giant on horseback as is the norm, but as an old man with a remarkably tiny head.

There is a strip of beach between the fortress walls and the Neva and here Petersburgers, sporting the latest in retro swimwear, begin to appear in mid-April or whenever the temperature rises above 10°C, standing up against the wall to shelter themselves from the wind and achieve maximum exposure to the sun. Here danger-seekers and other fools with toxic death-wishes can take a dip in the city waters of the Neva. Don't freak if you hear artillery fire: it's not the start of another coup - it just means that it's either noon or midnight or, at the very worst, a flood.

Metro: Gorkovskaya. Open 11:00-18:00 daily except Wed. Excursion bureau: 238 4540.

St. ISAAC'S CATHEDRAL

St. Isaac of Dalmatia was the patron saint of the Romanov family; little good he did them. Construction of the present version of St. Isaac's (there had been three previously which either sank into the mud or weren't big enough to be entirely satisfactory) took 40 years and was finally completed in the mid-19th century.

The cathedral is replete with colored marble, the fourth largest cupola in the world (coated with 100 kilos of gold), an enormous stained-glass Jesus, extravagantly sculptured bronze doors, burly mosaics and one of the few collections of icons that managed to stay intact through the Soviet era. Climb the colonnade (562 steps) for a panoramic view of the city, or to try to steal parts of the roof. Note that tickets to the colonnade are sold separately from tickets to the interior museum.

Isaakievskaya Ploshchad 1. Metro: Nevsky Prospekt then trolleys 5, 14 or 22, or 15 minute walk. Cathedral open 11:00-19:00, colonnade open 11:00-17:00 daily except Wed. Tel: 315 9732.

MUSEUM OF ETHNOGRAPHY

In reality this place should be titled "Museum of Ethnography and Blatant Soviet Propaganda" since the permanent exhibits trumpet Soviet-style international friendship and gratitude towards the Russian people from proletarian atheists of all races and, well, creeds. There are interesting exhibits of folk clothing from peoples of the Russian Federation as well as evocative photos, interesting wooden utensils and mock huts representing peoples who live in far out Siberian reaches where they have lots of words for "snow."

Inzhenernaya Ulitsa 4/1. Metro: Nevsky Prospekt. Open 10:00-18:00 daily except Mon and the last Fri of the month. Tel: 210 3888.

KUNSTKAMERA

The Kunstkamera, German for "Chamber of Art", houses the Museum of Anthropology and Ethnography (not to be confused with the Museum of Ethnography). Located across the Dvortsovy Bridge from the Winter Palace, the green and white, dome-capped Kunstkamera building was commissioned in 1718 by Peter the Great as the Academy of Sciences. He later placed here his collection of curiosities gathered during his foreign travels and established St. Petersburg's first museum. A legend of reputable authenticity says that in order to attract visitors admission was free and included a complimentary glass of vodka and slice of *salo* (see *Food and Drink*). Unfortunately both inducements have been done away with so you'll need to bring your own bottle and pay to get in. The museum features Peter's collection which includes a vital organ assortment, deformed fetuses, Siamese-twin infants, a two-faced cat and other oddities of questionable taste but undeniable interest. The entrance is from the side. *Fresh tip:* Time your visit here so that it is not right before lunch or dinner.

Universtiteskaya Naberezhnaya 3. Metro: Nevsky Prospekt then trolleys 1, 7 or 10 across the bridge. Open 11:00-16:45 Sun-Thur. Tel: 218 1412.

MARBLE PALACE

Catherine the Great ordered the Marble Palace to be built as a present for her lover, Count Orlov, who first had the nerve to lose it twice in card-games (both times Catherine bought it back and presented it to him anew) and then had the audacity to die before it was finished. Both the interior and exterior are fronted in 32 different kinds of marble, hence the name. Formerly home to the Leningrad branch of the Central Lenin Museum, it is now used for various temporary exhibitions and a new semi-permanent exhibition entitled "Formal Portraits of Russia".

Millionnaya Ulitsa 5/1. Metro: Nevsky Prospekt. Open 10:00-18:00 daily except Tues, 10:00-17:00 Mon. Tel: 312 9196.

KSHESINSKAYA MANSION

Before the Great October Socialist Revolution this stately mansion was the home of Matilda Kshesinskaya, the prima-ballerina of the Mariinsky Theater who was a lover of Nicholas II. Then for a long time it was a museum for the very same Great October Socialist Revolution that was so bad for Matilda's lover. Now it is a museum of Russian political history. They have a large exhibition of documents and photos and a St. Petersburg version of Madame Toussaud's (the exhibition is called "Russia: Terror or Democracy"). There is also a large stained-glass set of Socialist scenes in classic proletarian consciousness-raising style just inside the main entrance. If anywhere in the city barefaced Soviet propaganda still flourishes, it is here.

Ulitsa Kuibysheva 4. Metro: Gorkovskaya. Open 11:00-18:00 daily but most exhibitions closed Thur. Every Sat and the first and third Wed of the month there are evening concerts of chamber music. Tel: 233 7189, 233 7052.

KAZANSKY CATHEDRAL

Kazansky was built at the beginning of the 19th century during one of the many Russian-Turkish wars. Alexander I decided that building a large duplicate of St. Peter's in Rome would prove that Russia was a serious superpower that Turkey shouldn't mess with. Apparently it worked; the Turks surrendered before the cathedral's completion and it was decided not to build a southern colonnade to match the northern one facing Nevsky.

At the moment the **Museum of Religion** is housed here though its days here are numbered. In Socialist times the cathedral housed the ideologically-slanted Museum of Religion and Atheism. The rather graphic **Spanish Inquisition** exhibition is tucked away in the basement and, at least for a while, it can still be seen by special arrangement.

Field Marshal Mikhail Kutuzov, hero of the Napoleonic War, is buried in the cathedral and there are monuments to him and to General Mikhail Barclay de Tolli in Kazan Square facing Nevsky. Note that from a certain angle, General Barclay de Tolli seems to be doing something to himself that he shouldn't be doing in public; this is revenge on the randy general for sleeping with the sculptor's wife.

Kazanskaya Ploshchad 2. Metro: Nevsky Prospekt. Open 11:00-16:30 daily except Wed (from 12:00 Sat, Sun and during religious festivals). Tel: 311 0495.

PETER'S HOUSE
One of the oldest buildings in St. Petersburg, Peter's House was built in three days during 1703 close to the site of the Peter and Paul Fortress so that he could supervise its construction. Note that the ceilings here are only 2.5 meters high, which might seem strange as Peter was over 2 meters tall himself. Apparently he had a terrible fear of high ceilings, and if at any time during his trips abroad he was provided with a high-ceilinged room, he requested his hosts to rig up a lower false ceiling of cloth so he would be able to sleep. This museum is good for Peter the Great buffs, otherwise it's just an old house.

Across from the house on the banks of the Neva are the "Shih Tze" statues, half-lion and half-frog, which were brought here from Manchuria at the beginning of this century.

Petrovskaya Naberezhnaya 6. Metro: Gorkovskaya. Open 10:00-18:00 daily except Tues, closed Nov 11 to April 30. Tel: 238 9070.

MENSHIKOV PALACE

One of Peter I's closest pals was Prince Aleksander Menshikov. Born to non-aristocratic parents, his rise to prominence is owed to having befriended Peter in childhood. Peter bestowed the governorship of Petersburg upon Menshikov, and also that of Pushkin (Tsarskoye Tselo) which he later took back. Before Peterhoff was built, Peter held official functions and parties at Menshikov's place.

Catherine I, Peter's second wife, was originally a serving girl working for Menshikov. Menshikov knew how much Peter liked women, particularly other people's women, and so despite their good friendship he was reluctant to show this serving girl to the Tsar. Nonetheless, Peter was a crafty fellow and he managed to swoop the serving girl away from Menshikov. From there it was all grapes and roses for the girl who became Tsarina and even ruled the country for a couple of years after Peter's death. Menshikov's fate after Peter's death was not quite as fortunate. He and his family were packed off to Siberia after he over-asserted himself in an attempt to weasel into power. And people say there was no social mobility in pre-Revolutionary Russia. The palace itself is interesting as an illustration of how the nobility lived back then.

Universitetskaya Naberezhnaya 15. Metro: Vasileostrovskaya. Open 10:30-16:30 daily except Mon. Tel: 213 1112.

YUSUPOVSKY PALACE

The most sumptuous non-imperial palace in St. Petersburg was the home of the unabashedly rich and powerful Yusupov

Grigory Rasputin is without question one of the most scandalous figures in Russian history. This randy mystic from Siberia arrived in St. Petersburg in 1911 and within a few years became one of the most influential men in government circles. His ability to remain in such a high position despite widely publicized bouts of drinking and womanizing is no doubt the source of tremendous envy among political figures around the world today.

Rasputin's rise to preeminence was due to his close relationship with Nicholas II's wife, Alexandra. The heir to the throne, Alexis, suffered from hemophaelia, and only Rasputin could do what the top medical professors could not: he could stop the bleeding whenever there was an accident. Because of this, Alexandra believed he was a holy man sent to protect Alexis and she kept him close by at all times, despite the fact that he rarely bathed.

Rasputin is as famous for his death as he is for his life. At the end of 1916, a group of aristocrats in cahoots with the Grand Duke Dmitri Pavlovich (a cousin of Nicholas II) decided that Rasputin's influence had grown too great and that he had to be killed in order to save Russia. They lured him to the Yusupovsky Palace on the pretext that Prince Felix Yusupovsky would introduce Rasputin to his beautiful wife. Rasputin was led to the basement and fed poisoned cakes and wine, but these did not have any affect on him. Yusupovsky then shot the monk at point blank range and Rasputin collapsed on the floor. When Yusupov ran upstairs to tell his fellow conspirators the good news, they sent him back down to make sure he had done the job. On returning to inspect the body, Rasputin suddenly regained consciousness and started to throttle poor Yusupov, who needless to say was completely scared out of his wits. The Prince fled the basement, screaming for help; when they returned Rasputin was gone. They found him in the yard crawling towards the gate, where they proceeded to shoot and bludgeon him. They then tossed him into the river. When Rasputin was found, his lungs had filled with water, showing that he didn't actually die until he was submerged in the frozen waters.

family. However, the palace is not as famous for its elegant rooms, beautiful theater and what remains of its original art collection as it is for Grigory Rasputin's assassination which took place here in the winter of 1916. After the Revolution the building was transferred to the Teachers' Trade Union and has been remarkably well preserved. Standard tours are offered as well as a special "Death of Rasputin" tour, hyped to the fullest by over-dramatic tour guides.

Naberezhnaya Reki Moiki 94. Metro: Nevsky Prospect then buses 22 or 27, or a 20 minute walk. Admittance as part of a tour only; for reservations tel: 311 5353.

DOSTOEVSKY HOUSE/MUSEUM
If you want to get an idea of Dostoevsky's world, read his books. If you want to see a clean apartment with tacky wallpaper and a few not-so-interesting pieces of Dostoevsky memorabilia, spend the 20 minutes it takes to cruise through here. Much more interesting are their guided tours of places associated with Dostoevsky around town featuring a Crime and Punishment trek through the neighborhood where Raskolnikov lurked.

Kuznechny Pereulok 5/2. Metro: Vladimirskaya. Open 10:30-17:00 daily except Mon and the last Wed of the month. Tel: 164 6950.

PUSHKIN HOUSE/MUSEUM
Similar in principle to the Dostoevsky Museum and of interest mostly to local grade-school teachers and leaders of foreign exchange-student groups.

Naberezhnaya Reki Moiki 12. Metro: Nevsky Prospekt. Open 10:40-17:00 daily except Tues and the last Fri of the month. Tel: 311 3801.

THEATRICAL MUSEUM
A good choice for theater buffs or if the names Shalyapin, Stanislavsky or Meyerhold mean more to you than Larry, Moe

and Curly. There is also a collection of vintage theater costumes and props designed by *Mir Iskusstva* masters Benoir and Bakst.

Ploshchad Ostrovskogo 6. Metro: Gostiny Dvor. Open 11:00-18:00 daily except Tues, 13:00-19:00 Wed. Tel: 311 2195.

MUSEUM OF THE ARCTIC AND ANTARCTIC
Located in a former church. Try not to bump your head on the model plane hanging near the entry (you may not see it in the gloom). The plane represents that flown by the famous Soviet pilot Chkalov when he flew from Moscow to America via the North Pole. And the big stuffed polar bear represents why you shouldn't wander around the North Pole without a good supply of pointy sticks.

Ulitsa Marata 24-a. Metro: Mayakovskaya. Open 10:00-17:00 Wed-Sun. Tel: 311 2549.

MUSEUM OF MUSICAL INSTRUMENTS
They have a huge collection from around the world, most of which is kept locked away. If you ask nicely they may show you the hidden collection - one of the nice things about off-the-wall museums is the amount of individual attention a visitor receives (though they won't let you play the instruments).

Isaakievskaya Ploshchad 5. Metro: Nevsky Prospekt then trolleys 5, 14 or 22, or 15 minute walk. Open 12:00-18:00 daily except Mon and Tue. Tel: 314 5345.

ARTILLERY MUSEUM
One of Petersburg's oldest museum collections (founded in 1756) the museum exhibits weapons and military objects from 15th century firearms to ballistic missles. There are tanks, trucks and howitzers out front for the kiddies to play on.

Park Lenina 7 near the Peter and Paul Fortress. Metro: Gorkovskaya. Open 11:00-18:00 Wed-Sun. Tel: 232 0296.

MAJOR SIGHTS

One of the major highlights of St. Petersburg is the fantastic architecture and landscaping that abounds in the city center. The city was planned and built with the help of leading architects from all over the world, and the result is an eclectic mix of European and traditional Russian styles. Petersburg reminds some visitors of Rome, others of Paris, still others of Venice, Vienna or Amsterdam; elements of all these cities are here, yet at the same time it resembles none of them. You can spend weeks wandering around the center of the city and still find something new at every corner. Though the most convenient way to see the major sights is by car or transport, a good walk around Petersburg's older regions will give you more time to really take in the wondrous sights.

People who appreciate Petersburg's fine architecture should thank **Josef Stalin** that the historic city center has survived as well as it has. Other Russian cities, notably Moscow, had their architectural bases uprooted and replaced by big Stalinist-style buildings typical of mid-century Soviet architecture. Petersburg's palaces and pre-Revolutionary architecture were not systematically taken down and replaced by the type of buildings that abound on Moskovsky Prospekt and Prospekt Stachek ironically due to Stalin's personal hatred of Petersburg. Rather than do the undeserving city the favor of rebuilding it in the style of "developed socialism", he preferred to leave it to rot in peace.

PALACE SQUARE
Palace Square is one of the reasons St. Petersburg is frequently dubbed an open-air museum. On the north side stands the Winter Palace, a pearl of Russian baroque architecture. The big yellow semi-circular building opposite the Winter Palace, which houses the General Staff, was designed by Carlo Rossi

in the classical style. In the center of the square stands the Triumphal (or Alexander, as it is commonly known) Column. The 47.5 meter column was erected in 1834 in honor of the victory over Napoleon. The column is not secured to the ground and stands thanks to gravity alone, so if you're here during a really strong wind or an earthquake run for it.

The square has seen its fair share of important political events. In 1905 it was the site of the "Bloody Sunday" demonstration which marked the beginning of the first Russian revolution. The second and third revolutions also took place here, since the powers-that-be hung out in the Winter Palace. During the Bolsheviks' reign the square was a place for "peaceful demonstrations of solidarity" and military parades. Now, in the "democracy era," Palace Square is home to all kinds of political demonstrations - democrats, communists, monarchists, anarchists, anti-Zionists and so on gather here when they feel the need to engage in some collective shouting.

Metro: Nevsky Prospekt then a 15 minute walk or 2 stops on trolleys 1, 7 or 10.

NEVSKY PROSPEKT

If in Europe all roads lead to Rome then in St. Petersburg all roads lead to Nevsky. This 4.5 kilometer long avenue is the heart of St. Petersburg, teeming with life from early morning until late at night. Everything can be found on Nevsky - the best hotels, tons of restaurants and cafes, several movie theaters, shops, theaters and concert halls. Nevsky combines and compresses all of St. Petersburg onto one street; here one can see all the brilliance and all the squalor of the city. Newly renovated buildings stand next to decrepit and gutted ones, chic new Western retail shops are alongside State shops with huge crowds and bare shelves, and young currency speculators and peddlers of kitschy souvenirs share street space with beggars and musicians. Nevsky is the main cruising ground of mafiosi in their expensive wheels, irate nationalists and communist demonstrators, hare krishnas, leaflet pushers and anyone else who thrives on attention.

Nevsky is also one of Petersburg's most beautiful streets, a fact that amidst all the hubbub often gets overlooked. There are only three buildings that were built in the 20th century: the Aeroflot building (house #7), the Singer Sewing Company building (now *Dom Knigi*, house # 28) and house #14 upon which is written "Citizens! During shelling this side of the street is more dangerous," a relic from the Great Patriotic War. Three bridges span Nevsky - Politseisky Bridge over the Moika River, Kazansky Bridge over Kanal Griboyedova, and Anichkov Bridge with its four horse statues over the Fontanka. Nevsky is home to architectural gems like Kazansky Cathedral, Ploshchad Ostrovskogo (with a monument to Catherine the Great and the Alexander Theater), and the palaces of Stroganov (house #17), Anichkov (house #39) and Belozersky-Beloselsky (house #41).

Most of all, Nevsky is where it's at. Ever since it was first laid in 1710 it has been Petersburg's backbone, as much a symbol of the city as the Bronze Horseman and the Peter and Paul Fortress. A walk from the Admiralty to Ploshchad Vosstaniya takes about an hour and will expose you to the city's heart and soul.

STRELKA

The Strelka (or Spit) picturesquely lies on the edge of Vasilievsky Island overlooking both the Peter and Paul Fortress and the Winter Palace. The Neva is at its widest point here (1 km). The Strelka is bordered to the west by the Stock Exchange building, with a great Neptune statue on top. The Strelka was St. Petersburg's main port for over 100 years, with the big reddish Rostral columns serving as lighthouses. During festivities, flames alight the top of the columns and fireworks explode over the Neva. Hopefully the hoards of postcard and rabbit-hat wielding scruffy teenagers and their trombone-tooting pals will not detract too much from your enjoyment of one of Petersburg's most beautiful spots.

Across the bridge from the Hermitage. Metro: Nevsky Prospekt then 3 stops on trolleys 1, 7 or 10.

SENATE SQUARE

Between St. Isaac's Cathedral and the Neva lies this large square, formerly Decembrists' Square, the home of Falconet's famous **Bronze Horseman** statue. The statue, commissioned by Catherine the Great in honor of Peter the Great, is inscribed on the sides in Latin and Russian "To Peter the First from Catherine the Second." The piece of granite upon which the statue rests was a favorite of Peter the Great. Previously located in Lahta on the Gulf of Finland, Peter affectionately called it "thunder" and used to observe the surroundings from its top. Catherine had 400 people drag the enormous rock to St. Petersburg specifically to serve as the base for this statue. This monument has come to symbolize the city of St. Petersburg more than any other and it was a main character in both Pushkin's mini-epic about this city "The Bronze Horseman" and the symbolist Andrei Bely's surreal novel, <u>Petersburg</u>.

West of the Horseman stand the former Senate and Synod buildings, now housing historical archives. Across from them, to the east of the statue, is the **Admiralty**, one of Petersburg's first buildings. Senate Square was the sight of the ill-fated Decembrists' uprising in 1825. This event earned the square a new name during the Socialist era as the Decembrists were canonized in Communist propaganda as visionaries and precursors of socialism, which is about as historically sound as claiming that Brezhnev's precursor was Elvis.

Metro: Nevsky Prospekt then a 20 minute walk or trolleys 5, 14 or 22 to St. Isaac's Square.

SUMMER GARDENS and SUMMER PALACE

The Summer Gardens were designed by Peter I in 1704 who also planted its first trees. In addition to being a nice place for a stroll, Peter used the gardens as the location for some of his strange festivities called "assemblies". The Tsar would order aristocrats to gather here with their wives and children. His soldiers would lock the gates and stand guard to ensure nobody left early and then distribute vodka, wine and beer from huge barrels to all the guests whether they wanted it or not. It was considered a *faux pas* of extraordinary magnitude to refuse to drink to the Tsar's health and potentially quite dangerous to one's social position. At the end of the assembly those who could still manage to stagger would be free to go, their social position secure until the next assembly.

The statues (covered in the cold seasons) depict characters from Greek and Roman mythology as well as some other historical figures. The gardens are also the location of Peter's **Summer Palace**, built between 1710 and 1714, which show how humbly this tsar lived relative to the more opulent style of Catherine the Great whose house is not too far from here. In autumn, people and their pets stroll around wearing goofy hats woven out of golden leaves.

One of the main attractions of the Summer Gardens is the beautiful wrought-iron work on the railing bordering the Neva embankment. Legend says that a 19th century English

lord anchored his yacht in the Neva opposite the Summer Gardens. The lord, an art connoisseur, admired the black and gold grille then immediately set sail for England, remarking that he had accomplished the goal of his voyage and nothing could surpass the splendor of this sight. Hopefully you'll stay longer than this chump did.

Though the Summer Gardens close in the evening, it is not too difficult to hop the fence, and for years local youth would do so to hang out after hours. Nowadays this is probably not the brightest idea as sometimes after closing the authorities release patrols of German shepherds.

Gardens open 08:00-22:00 (until 20:00 in the cold seasons); Summer Palace open 11:00-19:00 from April 30 to November 10 daily except Tues. Metro: Gostiny Dvor then trams 2, 12 or 34; Metro: Gorkovskaya then bus 25, 46 or 134. Palace tel: 314 0374.

FIELD OF MARS

Formerly the *Poteshnoye pole* (old Russian for "Fun Field"), the Field of Mars came into being in 1710. Later, when Empress Elizabeth built her palace on the site of the present Engineer's Castle, the field came to be known as *Tsaritsyn lug* (literally "Tsarina's Meadow"). Paul I, a great lover of military formations, made it into military parade and training grounds, from which the name "Field of Mars" arose. During the 1917 February Revolution a bunch of people were heroically killed here which led the Bolsheviks (who never needed much encouragement to build monuments glorifying the Revolution) to construct the existing memorial and eternal flame and to rename the field "Victims' of the Revolution Square." The name did not catch on and after a few years the Square once again became a Field. The Bolsheviks buried here are less famous than those resting in Moscow's Red Square but were important enough to have had some factories and streets named after them.

Metro: Nevsky Prospekt or Gostiny Dvor then a 10 minute walk.

ENGINEER'S CASTLE

The Engineer's Castle, also known as the Mikhailovsky Castle, was commissioned by Paul I after the Archangel Michael came to him in a dream with the message to built a fortress at his birthplace. Paranoid Paul, fearing an assassination attempt, had the castle built at a furious pace and surrounded it with moats. His fears were justified as shortly after the castle's completion in early 1801 Paul was assassinated by his own guards in a palace coup. It is believed that Paul's son, Alexander I, approved the coup but tried to guarantee that his father would not be harmed. The conspirators, however, had overpartaken of the bottle to get their courage up and got carried away when Paul feebly resisted. After the assassination no member of the royal family would live here and it became a school of military engineering.

The castle, whose four façades are all different, is not a museum and theoretically people without any official business are not supposed to be crawling around inside, or around the totally zany courtyard. To the south of the castle is a statue of Peter I sitting on a horse who has a colossal *derrière*. Paul commissioned the monument, and it is inscribed "To great-grandfather from great-grandson".

Sadovaya Ulitsa 2 (across from the Summer Garden's south entrance). Metro: Gostiny Dvor then trams 2, 12 or 34; Metro: Gorkovskaya then bus 25, 46 or 134.

CHURCH OF THE BLEEDING SAVIOR

The moniker "Bleeding Savior" is somewhat arbitrary as this church has twenty different names depending on whom you ask. For some reason Bleeding Savior has stuck in most English-language tourist publications, winning out over "Resurrection of Christ", "Assumption", "Church of the Redeemer", and the nearly identical "Savior on the Spilled Blood". On this site a terrorist from the revolutionary organization *People's Will* mortally wounded Tsar Alexander II on March 1, 1881, by tossing a bomb at his feet. His son Alexander III began construction of the memorial church in 1883 and it was completed in 1907 during the reign of Nicholas II. The church was modelled after the over-photographed St. Basil's in Moscow's Red Square and its flamboyant Russian style can be attributed to a rise in national consciousness at the turn of the century. Scaffolding surrounded the church for over 40 years of renovation and only recently came down. Currently the church can only be enjoyed from the outside, though it will soon be opened to the public.

Located at the head of Kanal Griboyedova just off of Nevsky Prospekt. You can't miss it.

ALEXANDER NEVSKY LAVRA

Peter the Great founded the Lavra on the purported site of the legendary 1240 battle between Alexander Nevsky and the Swedes. The term Lavra is usually translated as monastery or abbey, and there are only four in all of Russia. The Metropolitan of the Orthodox Church resides here. (Metropolitans are second to the Patriarch in the Orthodox Church hierarchy.) Even during the Soviet period the Orthodox seminary continued to function here with only a few years' break. The **Holy Trinity Cathedral**, St. Petersburg's main functioning place of worship, is located here. Also worth seeing are two **cemeteries** filled with intricate monuments to the people resting here, including Dostoevsky, Tchaikovsky, Mussorgsky and other local luminaries of the 18th and 19th centuries.

Ploshchad Aleksandra Nevskogo. Metro: Ploshchad Alexandra Nevskogo. Cemeteries open 11:00-19:00 (in winter to 18:00) except Tues and Sat. Tel: 274 0409.

SMOLNY

The Empress Elizabeth commissioned Rastrelli to construct a convent where she planned on spending her last days. Alas Rastrelli, who was busy constructing both the Winter Palace and the Summer Palace in Tsarskoye Selo, did not finish it before the Empress' death and the convent was never completed. Catherine the Great, in her endless desire to inflict enlightenment upon her subjects, took what there was of the Smolny project and turned it into a finishing school for daughters of the gentry, the first educational establishment for women in Russia. The young women lived and studied in the long blue buildings flanking the cathedral. As the school expanded the neighboring yellow Smolny Institute was built to hold the overflow.

During the Civil War the beautiful cathedral was used as a vegetable warehouse and later closed while all the icons and other valuables were stripped out. It re-opened after World War II as the Museum of Leningrad - Today and Tomorrow exhibiting "the great contribution made by the people of Leningrad to the fulfillment of the resolutions of the Party and government". This too has closed and now Smolny is the home of temporary exhibitions and occasional choir or chamber concerts.

The Smolny Institute was also filled with vegetables for a long time - the rubber-stamp Council of People's Deputies worked here until 1989, receiving all their orders from the modern building just across Proletarian Dictatorship Square where the Leningrad Communist Party was housed. The institute now houses the offices of Mayor Sobchak and his administration and is not open to the public (though see page 144 for information on the **Lenin Museum**).

Ploshchad Rastrelli 3. Metro: Chernyshevskaya then trolleys 15, 18 or 49; Metro: Ploshchad Vosstaniya then trolleys 5 or 7. Cathedral open 11:00-17:00 daily except Thur. Tel: 271 9182.

THE TAURIDE GARDENS AND PALACE
This palace belonged to Count Grigory Potemkin of Tauria (the old name for the Crimea), another of Catherine the Great's lovers and one of the richest men in the country. After both Potemkin and Catherine died, Paul I (who detested everything associated with his mother) turned the sumptious palace into a cavalry barracks and horse stables.

After the October Manifesto in 1905 the palace was used for Duma sessions until the February Revolution, after which it was taken over by the Socialist Coalition of the Provisional Government. In 1918 the Constituent Assembly met here before being dissolved by armed Bolsheviks. The building was used during the Soviet period by the Communist Party as the Higher Party School and occasionally for weddings by renegade mayors. Watch your step in the gardens as it is where people take their doggies for walkies.

Metro: Chernyshevskaya and a five minute stroll to the east.

NEW HOLLAND
A 10 minute walk west of St. Isaac's Square will bring you to New Holland, an island formed by the Moika, Kryukov and Admiralteisky Canals. The red brick buildings were used to

store lumber for the Admiralty, and in the 19th century a boat and submarine testing pool was built on the island. The island is not open to the public, but this area is a picturesque and quiet part of the city center.

No close metro; best to walk from St. Isaac's Square along the Moika River.

THE CRUISER AURORA

This 19th century battleship will be of interest to lovers of kitschy revolutionary relics. The blank shot that signalled the start of the Revolution was fired from the cruiser's main gun. The next day Lenin announced the beginning of the communist era from its radio-cabin. Recent reconstruction has made the ship look like an oversized toy.

Admission is free. Petrogradskaya Naberezhnaya 4. Metro: Gorkovskaya. Open 10:30-16:30 daily except Mon and Fri.

CEMETERIES

There are a couple interesting cemeteries in St. Petersburg in addition to the necropolis in the Alexander Nevsky Lavra.

The **Piskarevskoye Cemetery** is where the almost 500,000 victims of the Second World War are buried. The mass graves marked only with the year, an eternal flame and a large Motherland statue remind visitors of the tremendous suffering and loss of life the city underwent during the blockade. *Prospekt Nepokoryonnykh 74. Metro: Ploshchad Muzhestva then buses 101 or 124.*

The **Smolenskoye Cemetery** on Vasilievsky Island is a beautiful and quiet place, as well as the home of the **Kseniya Peterburzhskaya Chapel**. People used to come here to write their requests on the chapel walls until the *perestroika* government found religion and gave the chapel back to the Church, who then canonized Kseniya as the patron saint of St. Petersburg and painted over all the messages. If you ask nicely they will give you a little gob of sacred oil which some people say cures absolutely everything. *Metro: Primorskaya then trolleys 10 or 46.*

SOVIET MEMORIALS AND MEMORABILIA

Although the Soviet Union no longer exists and Communism has been at least nominally disavowed, its 74 years left its mark on the face of the city. It is only a matter of time before all the Socialist statues and slogans are removed, the names changed and the plaques taken down (as has been the case throughout Eastern Europe) so if socialist kitsch turns you on at all, don't put it off until your next visit - photograph now.

Politically Active Statues
St. Petersburg celebrated its 290th birthday by replacing the phallic Lenin bust in the Moscow Train Station with a statue of Peter the Great, and it probably want be too long before the other Lenins are moved to museums or melted down to make metro tokens. Lenin buffs can see the slightly rotund Lenin in front of the **Warsaw Train Station** pointing the way to the city center. Outside the **Finland Train Station** is a stirring depiction of a speech V.I. Lenin gave after returning from Finland just after the February Revolution. The thing he is standing on is an armored car (alas the original is no longer displayed in the garden of the Marble Palace) and he is pointing across the river to a tall orange building with a large antenna - KGB headquarters. Perhaps the best Lenin is down on **Moskovsky Prospekt** in front of a classically nightmarish Stalin building where a 16 meter-tall Bad Vlad daintily proffers his cap to the proletariat. Traditionalists can see the statues of Marx and Engels in the park between the Smolny (where there is another fine Lenin statue as well) and Proletarian Dictatorship Square.

The Lenin Museum
Although the huge Central Lenin Museum is gone for good, there is a smaller museum in the Smolny dedicated to the once revered founder of the Soviet Union. The exhibition includes some great socialist-realist portraits of Lenin, Stalin and other Revolutionary heroes.

In the Smolny Institute. Admittance by pre-arranged excursion only, call at least one day in advance. Open 10:00-17:00 Mon-Fri, 11:00-15:00 Sat. Tel: 278 1461.

Monument to the Heroic Defenders of Leningrad
This large monument greets travellers arriving from the airport or coming in by car from the south. Unveiled on V-E day in 1975, the monument feature classic socialist-style statues of soldiers and civilians in dramatic poses as well as a somber under-ground museum dedicated to the plight of Leningrad during the war.

Ploshchad Pobedy. Metro: Moskovskaya then a ten minute walk or one stop south on any bus or trolley.

The Metro
The history of the metro dates back to the time of Tsar Alexander I when an engineer came to the Tsar with the idea of digging a tunnel from the center of the city to Vasilievsky Island. The Tsar responded by ordering him "not to engage in any hare-brained schemes in the future." This hare-brained scheme proved more durable than tsarism, and in 1955 the Kirovsky-Vyborgskaya (red) line opened with eight stations. Three other lines were to follow and currently construction on the Pravoberezhnaya (yellow) line is underway with several new stations planned for the northwest areas of the city.

St. Petersburg's Metro is not nearly as pompous and obtrusive as the one in Moscow, and for the most part it exemplifies function over form. Still, some of the oldest stations embody the concept of the metro as "people's palaces" and are crammed to the hilt with Communist propaganda and self-glorification. The hammer-and-sickle theme is frequent, along with bronze stars, laurel wreaths, industrial tools and wheat stalks set on imposing marble walls.

Several stations boast funky mosaics, like **Vladimirskaya** (depicting the abundance of happy Socialist life), **Baltiiskaya** (the cruiser Aurora firing on the Winter Palace), **Ploshchad Lenina** (humungus Vladimir Lenin greeting people as they leave the escalator), and **Avtovo** (Mother Country). Look carefully at the bronze wheels on the arches in **Ploshchad Vosstaniya** and you will see depictions of Lenin delivering one of his interminable speeches. **Narvskaya** is laden with consciousness-raising statuettes of soldiers, peasants and intellectuals in dramatic poses. **Kirovsky Zavod** is noteworthy for its canonization of the industrial world, a reminder that the Kirov Factory was the most revolutionary of revolutionary factories. The idea behind **Avtovo** was to use it as an underground palace of sorts where the people could party at officially organized festivities during the 50s. The more modern stations tend to be pretty boring, though **Mayakovskaya** boasts neo-1960s Chinese restaurant decor, and a depiction of tsarist troops suppressing a demonstration alights the top of the escalator at **Gostiny Dvor**.

Soviet architecture

Given the beauty of St. Petersburg's pre-Revolutionary architecture, Soviet architects attempting to beautify the city landscape had a tough act to follow. In Moscow they took care of that problem by tearing down a large portion of the city's historical center and erecting yellowish Stalinist slabs and Neanderthalish wedding-cake monstrosities in their wake. Fortunately this method was not applied to St. Petersburg. Instead, Soviet architects built up the outskirts of the city based on a concept of beauty which was redefined every couple of decades. Eventually they arrived at the ultimate architectural conclusion: the huge faceless concrete slab, as can be seen all throughout the former Soviet Bloc. For a real trip into the Twilight Zone, take a drive through ultra-new regions like **Leninsky Prospekt, Rzhevka, Kupchino** or the edge of Vasilievsky Island by **Primorskaya Metro**.

Moskovsky Prospekt, the street leading from the airport to the center, provides an excellent architectural retrospective spanning two centuries. The area closest to the airport has been built up in the last two decades and, judging by the quality of construction, will probably be down again in another two. Past the War memorial begins the late Stalinist age, known for powerful block forms (including square balconies and pillars), stone towers and huge imposing archways. Behind these buildings you can often find the mass-produced Khrushchev-era buildings, or *Khrushchovki* as they are condescendingly dubbed. These five-storey grey brick buildings, typified by their low ceilings and small rooms, were a part of Khrushchev's drive in the late 50s and early 60s to provide everyone with their own living space. Soviet architecture more or less ends and pre-Revolutionary begins when you cross Obvodny Kanal which was the pre-Revolutionary southern city limit.

FAR OUT

Within 50 kilometers south and west of St. Petersburg lie five groups of former tsarist estates. Most of them were devastated in World War II when the Nazis applied the loot-and-detonate strategy during the occupation. Restoration work began immediately after the War and the main palaces have largely been put back together again, though many secondary pieces still lie in ruins.

If you are not travelling by car, the way to reach these destinations is by electric train (*elektrichka*). Petrodvorets and Lomonosov can also be reached by **hydrofoil** from May until September. Hydrofoils leave from in front of the Hermitage for Petrodvorets and from Naberezhnaya Makarova near the Tuchkov Bridge for Lomonosov as well as Petrodvorets. Lines can be long, so go early and buy a return ticket.

These places all make good day trips. Either you can do it yourself or go with a tour booked through a hotel service bureau. If lunch is not included it's probably a good idea to bring your own as there may be little available there.

PUSHKIN

Located 25 kilometers south of St. Petersburg, the town of Pushkin (formerly Tsarskoye Selo) came into existence when Catherine I built a little surprise palace here for her husband Peter the Great. The Empress Elizabeth had the palace (named *Yekaterininsky Dvorets*, or **Catherine's Palace**) expanded and renovated in 1752 and work continued through Catherine the Great's reign. The 300 meter long palace was completely devastated during the War and restoration is not yet complete; pictures inside show its state after the German retreat. The palace housed the famous Amber Room, whose amber wall panels were stripped by the Nazis and are probably now in Paraguay.

Surrounding the palace are parks covering over 570 hectares (1400 acres) peppered with bridges, terraces, fountains and small galleries. Of note is the **Agate Pavilion** just southeast of the palace. A little way north of the palace is the **Alexander Palace** built for the future Alexander I at the end of the 18th century which is unfortunately closed to the public. Pushkin is also the sight of the Lyceum where Pushkin himself studied from 1811 to 1817, thus the old school houses the inevitable **Pushkin Museum**.

Park open 09:00-20:00 daily. Catherine's Palace open 11:00-18:00 (until 17:00 in non-summer months) daily except Tues and the last Mon of the month. Pushkin Museum open 11:00-17:00 daily except Tues. Elektrichka from Vitebsky Vokzal to the Pushkin station, then take bus 371 to the park.

PAVLOVSK

Named after Paul I, Pavlovsk was the last of the imperial palace complexes to be built. The grounds were given to Paul I by his mother Catherine the Great in 1777 on the occasion of the birth of the future Tsar Alexander I. Ransacked in World War II, Pavlovsk has been fully restored. The main feature is the **Grand Palace** (*Bolshoi Dvorets*), built from 1782 to 1786 and expanded during 1796 to 1799. The 1500 hectare (3750 acre) park contains several pavilions, notably the **Temple of Friendship** and the **Pavilion of the Three Graces**.

Park open 09:00-20:00 daily. Grand Palace open 10:00-18:00 daily except Fri and the first Mon of the month, only the State Rooms are open Thur. Pavilions open 10:30-16:30 daily June to October. Elektrichka from Vitebsky Vokzal to the northwest corner of the park, a 10 minute stroll from the palace.

PETRODVORETS

The history of Petrodvorets (called Peterhof until 1944) began in 1704 when Peter I built a wooden house on the Gulf while overseeing the construction of the nearby Kronstadt fortress.

In 1713 he began to transform the area into an imperial residence. The palace was inaugurated in 1723 and was later expanded by Empress Elizabeth. Petrodvorets is also a monument to Soviet reconstruction as the place was looted and razed almost completely by Nazi troops.

The **Grand Palace** (*Bolshoi Dvorets*) dominates the estate. Similar in scale to Catherine's Palace in Pushkin, it is filled with lavish rooms and galleries, some of which are rather bizarre thematically (like the Chesma Hall which features endless artistic renditions of the Russian victory over the Turks at Chesma Bay). The park ensemble contains the cozy **Monplaisir Palace** where Peter I preferred to live and which includes the Catherine Wing where Catherine the Great bided her time while conspirators removed her husband from the throne in 1762, as well as the **Chateau de Marly**, a former guesthouse in the Louis XIV style, and the **Hermitage Pavilion**, a highbrow two-storey dining room where guests sitting on the upper floor ate and drank in peace, occasionally lowering the table to the ground floor where servants did their thing (refilled wine glasses, replaced dirty plates, spat in the beef stroganoff, etc.).

There are 144 fountains in the parks, all operating without the use of pumps by a combination of naturally generated water pressure and magic. The **Upper Park** has as its centerpiece the Neptune Fountain which was originally built for the Nürnberg Marktplatz and never used, ending up here after Paul I bought it during one of his shopping trips to Germany. The **Lower Park** is the location of the famous Great Cascade which includes the Samson Fountain with a great spewing lion. The fountain commemorates the victory over the Swedes in 1709 on St. Samson's Day. Beware while walking around the Lower Park as there are several trick fountains that will spray an innocent passerby for the mere mistake of stepping on a funny stone or sitting on the wrong bench. East of the Lower Park lies the 19th century **Alexandria Park,** built for Nicholas I and named after his wife. It includes a neo-Gothic chapel, a farm house where Alexander II lived, and a cottage.

Parks open from 09:00-20:00 daily, the fountains operate from 11:00-20:00 (until 21:00 on Sun) from the last Sunday in May to the end of September. All museums open from 11:00-18:00. The Grand Palace is closed Mondays and the last Tuesday of each month; Chateau de Marly is closed Tuesdays and the last Wednesday of each month; Monplaisir and the Hermitage Pavilion are closed Wednesdays and the last Thursday of each month; the Cottage is closed on Fridays. A curse on whoever thought up this system. Elektrichka from Baltiisky Vokzal to Novy Petergof then buses 350, 351, 353 or 356 to the Fontana stop; access also by hydrofoil.

GATCHINA

45 kilometers southwest of St. Petersburg, Gatchina was first built by Count Grigory Orlov, one of Catherine the Great's lovers. After his death it became an imperial residence and the favorite of Paul I, who lived most of his life here. Western tourists were not allowed here for a long time as there was an institute for nuclear physics here and military installations nearby. The park ensemble, originally designed in the English style, has not yet completely recovered from the World War II devastation and is thus missing the Disneyland feel of Pushkin and Petrodvorets. The palace has been partially restored.

Open 11:00-17:00 daily except Mon and the first Tues of the month. Elektrichka from Baltiisky Vokzal to Gatchina-Baltiiskaya, about a one hour ride. Excursion bureau: (271) 13492.

LOMONOSOV

10 kilometers west of Petrodvorets, this estate was begun by Prince Menshikov who envied Peter's work on his seaside palace and wanted one as well, but the palace was not finished by the time Menshikov went bust and was shipped off to Siberia. It was further developed by Peter III and Catherine the Great. The palace and park was originally called Orienbaum, as Menshikov grew orange trees here in hot-houses.

Lomonosov is significantly less touristy and lower-key than Pushkin, Pavlovsk and Petrodvorets and is also the only estate to escape War damage. The **Grand Palace** (the upper-crusties before the Revolution were rather unimaginative in naming their palaces) has been closed for renovation for some time but it should re-open soon. All that remains of **Peterstadt,** where Peter III used to play, is the gateway and spire. Check out the **Katalnaya Gorka Pavilion**, an 18th century ski-lodge / roller-coaster starting point of sorts and the **Chinese Palace**, Baroque on the outside, Rococo on the inside with no real connection to China at all.

Open only in summer. Park open 09:00-22:00 daily, museums 11:00-18:00 (17:00 Mon) daily except Tues and the last Mon of the month. Elektrichka from Baltiisky Vokzal, a one hour ride to Orienbaum I station; access also by hydrofoil.

RAZLIV
A must for diehard Lenin buffs. Here in July and August, 1917, Vladimir Ilyich took refuge from the Provisional Government after the disastrous "July Days", Lenin's premature putsch. He shaved his moustache, donned a wig and lived for a while in the barn of Nikolai Yemelyanov, a Bolshevik worker from nearby Sestroretsk. After a short time he moved across the lake to a haystack, built especially for him by Yemelyanov. The tactics worked; the Provisional Government couldn't find the noodle in the haystack. Both barn and 'stack are museum pieces for the time being.

Open 10:00-18:00 daily except Wed. Elektrichka from Finlandsky Vokzal in the direction of Sestroretsk, get off at Razliv.

FARTHER OUT

If you have time it may be well worthwhile to take a cruise up the Neva. Cruises operate from around mid-May until October and are stylish ways to reach places such as **Kizhi, Valaam** and the **Solovetskiye Islands**. Cruises also go to and from Moscow during the warm months and are an excellent way to see the wild Russian countryside and small villages that haven't changed too much in the last few centuries.

Valaam

This picturesque archipelago is situated in the northern part of Lake Ladoga. The islands feature several ancient churches and mini-monasteries in a fantastic natural setting. The clean air and water are a welcome change from stuffy Petersburg, thus the cruises are filled with people seeking to get away from it all for a little drinking and carousing in the wild. There are designated camping sites on some of the islands.

Kizhi

This peninsula is first and foremost an open-air museum of wooden architecture. Wooden structures have been brought here from the region around Lake Onega, including some cute little peasant houses (*izba*) and several churches. The island boasts an interesting icon collection, though the most famous relic on Kizhi is the much-photographed 22-cupolad wooden **Church of the Transfiguration** that was built without nails. People tired of inhaling second-hand smoke will be glad to hear that Kizhi is a no-smoking zone.

You can use St. Petersburg as your base to get to Kizhi, or else head to the town of **Petrozavodsk** and take a boat from there. Located on the southwest shore of Lake Onega, this depressing industrial town's only merits are that it is convenient to Kizhi and that Ben & Jerry's have built a factory and retail their phantasmagorical ice cream here for rubles.

Solovetskiye Islands

This archipelago of six large and countless smaller islands is situated in the Gulf of Onega in the White Sea. Renown as the site of one of the first *gulags* set up by the Bolsheviks, the history of the islands is in fact quite a bit older. There are a number of ancient pagan burial sites as well as monasteries and other structures dating from the 16th century. Until being kicked out in the 1920s the community that lived here was entirely self-sufficient and legend has it that their vast treasure of religious artifacts remains buried. Declared a museum in 1967, the beautiful forest-covered islands are connected by a system of dams, bridges and canals and include a well-preserved 17th century fortress, churches and a small fishing village.

How to Get There
The City Excursion Bureau has cruises to Kizhi and Valaam two or three times per month. The Valaam cruise is a standard two days and one night deal. *Naberezhnaya Krasnogo Flota 56. No nearby metro. Tel: 311 4019.*

Sputnik cruises to Valaam and Kizhi. The Valaam cruise happens every summer weekend and is a two-day/one-night affair. They can provide translators if necessary. The Kizhi cruise lasts five days and includes stops in Valaam and Petrozavodsk. It runs only in the end of May and in September and October. *Ulitsa Chapygina 8. Metro: Petrogradskaya. Tel: 234 9808.*

CULTURE

Discussing culture in St. Petersburg is problematic for several reasons. As the city was conceived to be a window on the West through which Russia could adopt and adapt certain aspects of Western life, it would be somewhat farcical to call St. Petersburg a center of Russian culture. Petersburg is a combination of Europe with a Russian twist and Russia with a European twist, and as such it personifies Russia's perennial identity crisis as a country belonging neither to the East nor the West. This identity crisis, brought on by Peter the Great's bold reforms and dogging Russia throughout her history, continues to express itself today in the political struggle between reformist leaders who want to integrate Russia into the world community and nationalist ideologues who think Russia should "go her own way". Strange, since last time Russia boldly went her own way in 1917 the end result was Brezhnev. Which brings us to the point of this chapter: should you go to the ballet, or just have a few beers in the park?

The most common way to take in Petersburg's cultural offerings is to spend every day going to museums and every night going to ballets, operas, classical music concerts and other things commonly considered "high culture" (yawn). Indeed it is quite easy to sink into this routine, since St. Petersburg has more worthy museums than you can shake a stick at and is a world-renown performing arts center. What's more, for those who can only take so much of Swan Lake and Rachmaninov recitals, there exists a number of other cultural venues.

Tickets

Tickets for performances can generally be bought at ticket booths (театральная касса) throughout the city or inside the theaters themselves. The largest ticket booth in the city is at *Nevsky Prospekt 42*. Note that the availability of good tickets to prestigious shows is severely limited and the best seats are

usually not sold in normal booths but rather for hard currency by hotel service bureaus, tourist agencies and speculators. An increasing number of theaters have officially instituted price discrimination policies similar to those in museums, meaning that foreigners will not be admitted to see the show unless they purchased a special **hard currency ticket**.

15-day repertoires of all the major theaters are posted in the ticket booths. If you want to find out what is playing and can't figure out these schedules, ask any hotel service bureau or concierge desk for help. Before the institution of special hard currency tickets took the business out of their hands, flocks of scalpers used to hang out in front of popular theaters selling cheap ruble tickets for grossly inflated prices. They may still be there, trying to make a quick buck at the expense of some unsuspecting tourist who isn't aware of the hard currency ticket rule. Before buying anything from a scalper be sure that the theater does not have this rule or you will just end up making a gratuitous donation to some speculator.

Seating
Tickets have all kinds of strange things written on them describing where it is you're supposed to sit. Elevation is

marked by either партер (ground floor), белэтаж (next floor up), and ярус or балкон (balcony). Левая сторона means left side, Правая сторона means right. Места за креслами literally means "behind the seats" and usually signifies standing-room-only, or just before the show begins someone might produce some creaky chairs for you. If you're confused a theater employee can lead you to your seats. Ticket scalpers love to produce little maps of the theater and explain that the 5th ярус seats he has for $20 each are actually front-row center.

Etiquette
Russians attending nicer events (ballets, operas, philharmonic shows and the like) tend to dress up in their evening best so wearing shorts and thrashed t-shirts will only attract scornful looks from the public and harsh words from the employees. You can get away with wearing jeans and sneakers, though you will look like a slob. You must check your coat and larger bags upon entry. Photography during the show is absolutely forbidden, and if you fall asleep try not to snore too loudly as it may keep others awake.

OPERA AND BALLET

Ballet is an important part of St. Petersburg's cultural tradition and at the center of this is the world-renown Vaganova Ballet School. Founded in 1738, the extremely competitive Vaganova (there are only about 18 people in a class) matriculates world-class dancers every year. Contemporary ballet in Petersburg tends to be on the conservative side, though in recent years there have been some semi-spirited attempts to bust out and do something innovative. As many leading dancers have the chance to go abroad and dance with leading Western troupes, they are coming back with new ideas and techniques which will undoubtedly be integrated into the romantic-classical style that now prevails. The repertoire consists mostly of proven standards like "Swan Lake"

(Лебединое озера), "The Nutcracker" (Щелкунчик), "Giselle" (Жизель) and "Sleeping Beauty" (Спяшая красавица).

Opera also occupies an important part in Petersburg's cultural tradition. As in Europe, 19th century Petersburg aristocrats used to go to the opera and check each other out with opera glasses before leaving at intermission. The 19th century was also a prolific period for Russia's greatest opera writers. Leading the way was Tchaikovsky, who set Pushkin's epic poem "Eugene Onegin" (Евгений Онегин) and the story "The Queen of Spades" (Пиковая дама) to music. Mussorgsky's "Boris Godunov" (Борис Годунов), an operatic history of Russia's first dynastic crisis, was also penned in this time. If you plan on going to the opera, it is most likely you will hear one of these three as they run over and over again in all the theaters.

The Mariinsky Theater (formerly the Kirov) is an exquisite building that features one of the best ballet troupes in the world. The troupe, which performs only classical ballets, goes on tour every summer for about two months and often disappears during the year as well. The opera company is also quite famous, performing international favorites as well as Russian operatic classics. As the Mariinsky is *numero uno* in the city as far as cultural destinations are concerned, tickets can be hard to come by, particularly for ballets, though there are plenty of hotel service bureaus, tourist organizations and speculators more than happy to help you in this department. *Teatralnaya Ploshchad 1. Metro: Sadovaya then a 15 minute walk. Tel: 114 1211.*

The **Maly Opera and Ballet Theater** is to the Mariinsky what Tom Cruise is to Marlon Brando. Tourists are often herded here, and if they don't know better they may think that they saw quite a professional show. Good for people who just have to have an opera or ballet fix, or when the Mariinksy is on one of their frequent world tours. *Ploshchad Iskusstv 1. Metro: Nevsky Prospekt. Tel: 314 3758.*

There are also a couple of free-floating ballet troupes that don't have their own permanent stages. Performances are indicated on posters (in Russian, of course) hung around town, in ticket booths and in hotel service bureaus. The **St. Petersburg Theater of Ballet,** under the direction of Boris Eifman (a graduate of the Vaganova School) claims to be a modern ballet troupe, though it takes a rather conservative approach to modern dancing. The **Russian Ballet** troupe takes advantage of the Mariinsky's absence in the summer to inflict its mediocre performances on hapless guests to St. Petersburg who have heard just how great ballet is here.

CLASSICAL MUSIC

Petersburg is and has always been a major European center for classical music. Big shots like Rachmaninov, Tchaikovsky, Mussorgsky, Prokofiev, Rimsky-Korsakov and Shostakovich all lived and composed here. Some of them even decomposed here and are buried in the Alexander Nevsky Monastery (see *Sights*). Special music schools set Russian kids on the musical path at a young age (4 or 5 years old). Students from all over the world flock to the Conservatorium and a diploma from here is considered quite prestigious amongst classical music wonks. Every June during the **White Nights Festival** orchestras, chamber ensembles and soloists come to Petersburg to perform.

Tickets to classical performances are easier to obtain than ballet or opera tickets as they are less in demand, though if there is a special performance it may be necessary to resort to paying hard currency. The best place to check is the ticket booth at *Nevsky Prospekt 42*.

The **Shostakovich Philharmonic Hall** (also called the *Bolshoi Zal*, or Big Hall). The St. Petersburg Academic Orchestra, which due to emigration is a shadow of its former greatness, performs here as well as various other groups and soloists. Every now and then a travelling orchestra will perform here too, and tickets for these performances are quite difficult to come by. Before the Revolution this building was a meeting place for the *Boyar* Council (leading aristocratic families) and thus the acoustics, though adequate, are not fantastic. In addition to evening concerts there are sometimes less formal daytime performances on weekends. *Mikhailovskaya Ulitsa 2. Metro: Nevsky Prospekt. Tel: 311 7333.*

The cozier **Glinka Maly Zal** (Small Hall), as part of the philharmonic complex, also has fine concerts and the acoustics here are better than in the *Bolshoi Zal*, as it was designed specifically for performances. *Nevsky Prospekt 30. Metro: Nevsky Prospekt. Tel: 312 4585.*

Concerts are held in the **Conservatorium**, just across the square from the Mariinsky Theater. Student ballets and operas are performed in the Opera Hall, and they have a *Maly Zal* of their own where on Sunday mornings at 10:00 student concerts and open rehearsals are held. *Teatralnaya Ploshchad 3. Metro: Sadovaya then a 15 minute walk. Tel: 312 2519.*

The **Capella** houses a small concert hall where one can hear recitals, small orchestras, choirs and solo performances. The house choir sings the Sunday services in the Preobrazhensky Cathedral. *Naberezhnaya Reki Moika 20. Metro: Nevsky Prospekt. Tel: 233 0243.*

It has also become quite trendy to hold evenings of chamber music in various museums and palaces around town such as in *Dvorets Kompozitorov* at *Ulitsa Gertsena 45* and in the Kshesinskoi, Belozersky-Beloselsky and Yusupovsky palaces (see *Museums* and *Sights*). These are advertised on posters around the city and entry is usually either free or for a nominal sum.

For those who get a kick out of **folk music**, there is a folk center called **Terem** that has occasional concerts. These events are publicized by posters and pamphlets, and hotel service bureaus can arrange tickets. *In the "Palace of Labor"* (Дворец Труда). *Ploshchad Truda 4, room 78. No nearby metro. Tel: 219 8333.*

FILM

Looking at the film offerings around town can make one hanker for the good old days of censorship when trashy American films were categorically forbidden. In the last few years Russia has become the dumping ground for cheap Western flops heavy on the sex and violence and light on everything else, and finding something worthwhile is practically impossible. That's not all; foreign films are mercilessly dubbed into Russian, usually with one voice reading all the parts. Trying to glean the original dialogue behind the dubbing requires concentration that detracts from the film's enjoyment and even then you're unlikely to hear more than half the original dialogue. In a worst case scenario there will be a live dubber who stands near the screen with a microphone and gets tongue-twisted at the most important parts.

Still, if you speak Russian and look hard enough you can find some excellent Russian and Soviet films. These are shown with great rarity on the movie theater circuit; check newspapers like Час Пик, Пятница or Телевидение, Радио, Кино for listings. The **Spartak Theater** at *Ulitsa Saltykova-Shchedrina 8* is a revival-movie house, showing the best of old Russian and Soviet films as well as Western classics. Before the film a bespectacled grey-haired man talks for about 15 minutes about the artist, the world of film in general, his recent surgery and a whole series of unrelated subjects.

ROCK AND POP

> FRESH NOTE: This section is based on the Russian premise that "pop" and "rock" stand for two different phenomena. "Rock" covers a wide variety of music that emphasizes lyrical content and sound and in its more extreme forms, frenzied energy. "Pop" refers to flashy, image-oriented dance music heavy on the beat and light on lyrical content, musicality and variety.

Myth has it that all forms of popular music were perceived by zealous Soviet Cultural Ministry authorities as imperialist decadent propaganda and all of its vestiges mercilessly persecuted. This is not exactly true. Starting in the early 1970s, these authorities allowed pop music to develop, seeing it as a non-threatening form of modern music with its happy-go-lucky lyrics and feel-good beat. A select few musicians were even officially vilified so that young people could have objects of hero-worship with more rhythm than Lenin. Russian pop is a most unfortunate creation, being often little more than the same folk song chord structures over and over again set to a thumping synthesized beat and garnished with inane, whiny lyrics. Today's pop has taken a techno-house slant and musicians work harder on their image and dance steps, sloppily plagiarized from MTV videos.

Western musicians were represented in the Soviet Union almost exclusively by celebrities of the Eastern European stage, such as Bulgarian megastars Lili Ivanova and Biser Kirov and Polish groups called "Skaldy" and "The Red Guitars" who sang poppy Beatles-esque songs in Polish. Occasionally a Western group would be deemed acceptable by the authorities and would get some airplay, which led to the overblown popularity of groups like Boney M, the Bee Gees, Modern Talking and ABBA. One of the sad results of this bizarre censorship is that these four groups can still be heard on the airwaves here after years of virtual banishment in the West.

On the other hand, the Ministry of Culture did not recognize rock as a legitimate form of music with its anti-establishment lyrics and associations with drugs, decadence and free thought. Only here, rather than scold people for listening to or playing such music, they persecuted them for spreading "imperialist infections", withholding stipends, expelling them from institutes and universities and firing them from work. They even went so far as to pick up hippies off the street and forcibly cut their hair.

As a result, the vast majority of people had little exposure to rock music until relatively recently. Since materials to make and distribute bootleg copies of prized albums and tapes were almost nonexistent, people were forced to think up ways to spread the forbidden music around. The most common method before the advent of tape decks was to fashion make-shift records out of old x-ray photographs, affectionately known as records "on bones."

Rock began to crawl out of the underground in the early 80s, well before *perestroika* brought it to where it is now. State radio began to pepper propaganda broadcasts with the occasional rock song and an officially sanctioned rock club opened in Leningrad for rehearsals and performances. The musical iron curtain rose for good in the late 80s and early 90s, and commercial radio has made all the phases of Western music from the twist to disco to the latest hits available to listeners in Moscow, Petersburg and a host of other cities across the former Soviet Union.

Concerts
Concerts are advertised on the radio and by posters around town. Tickets are sold in random ticket booths. Common places for concerts are:

October Concert Hall - *Ligovsky Prospekt 6. Metro: Ploshchad Vosstaniya. Tel: 277 6960.*

SKK (Sports and Concert Complex that for a long time was named after V.I. Lenin) - *Prospekt Gagarina 8. Metro: Park Pobedy. Tel: 298 4847.*

Lensoviet Palace of Culture - *Kamennostrovsky Prospekt 42. Metro: Petrogradskaya. Tel: 233 8554, 233 8908.*

"Yubileiny" Palace of Sport - *Prospekt Dobrolyubova 18. Metro: Gorkovskaya. Tel: 238 4049.*

LDM Palace of Youth - *Ulitsa Professora Popova 47. Metro: Petrogradskaya. Tel: 234 3278.*

For a listing of rock and jazz clubs see *Nightlife*.

A Few Bands of Interest

Akvarium - Though they're old hat now, this Petersburg group was number one here for a long time and bandleader Boris Grebenshikov is the Elvis of Petersburg's rock scene.

Kino - Stretches the definitions of music, but nonetheless martyred bandleader Viktor Tsoi unites intelligentsia and young meatheads alike because of his clever lyrics and simple tunes.

Stranniye Igry - Schizophrenic lyrics set to neo-punk music, somewhat reminiscent of Fishbone.

Televizor - Music of the glasnost generation ("your daddy is a fascist" and so on).

Dva Samolyota - Great dance music à la Red Hot Chili Peppers. Their shows attract Petersburg's hipsters and yups.

Alisa - Not so much music as concentrated energy that drives teeny-boppers and aspiring hooligans into a frenzy.

DDT - One of the older and most popular groups, they manage to play very accessible music which successfully combines Russian folk and classic rock motifs.

NIGHTLIFE

Nightlife in St. Petersburg still shows the scars of 74 years of Communist oppression when most forms of organized fun were either outlawed or heavily restricted, meaning that a viable infrastructure of clubs, bars and other venues could not develop. A lack of places where people could gather and party down left them with little else to do but get together in each other's apartments and drink heavily. Over the past few years this major infrastructural gap has started to be filled, though there is still quite a long way to go. Price barriers keep the vast majority of the young and restless population away from hip bars, discos and clubs, and the ones that are cheap and accessible tend to attract teeny-boppers or lumpen alcoholics desperately in search of some place to go. Still, more and more socially active people are making and spending money and the current nightlife scene is a far cry from the drab days of yore.

One of the unfortunate realities of modern day St. Petersburg is that a lot of the people who have disposable income and the desire to get down 'n funky are bandits and *mafiosi*. Though a relaxing bandit may not be as obtrusive as when he's on the job, groups of drunken goons are never a pleasant sight and their concept of relaxing sometimes involves beating up on people they outweigh or outnumber. Often what happens to popular night spots is that sooner or later a group (or groups) of thugs choose it as their place to hang out and the atmosphere subsequently goes down the tube. It is impossible to say if today's hip club is tomorrow's gangster haven or vice versa but you'll know when you walk in the door, plus word of mouth travels pretty fast on such matters amongst the foreign community.

Hotels and Restaurants
Every **hotel** in town has some kind of bar or nightclub, and many restaurants gradually turn into hot night spots as the

evening progresses. The atmosphere (and prices) corresponds to that of the restaurant or hotel itself - older businessmen frequent fancy hotel nightclubs, a younger and more ethnically mixed crowd flocks places like Sadko's on weekend nights when they either have live music or wheel out the *karaoke* machine (much to the chagrin of the sober and those who aren't hearing impaired), and a wide cross-section of relaxing natives head to large ruble restaurants where there may be live "music", a variety show and/or gambling.

Night Clubs

The Landskrona, on the eighth floor of the Nevskij Palace Hotel, is a roof-top night restaurant featuring Russian and Continental cuisine and a full bar. International bands play dance music and there is an open-air terrace with a panoramic view over central St. Petersburg. *Nevsky Prospekt 57. Metro: Mayakovskaya. Open 19:00-01:00 Wed-Sun. Hard currency, major credit cards accepted. Tel: 275 2001.*

Joy This Nigerian-Russian-Swedish joint venture has created a truly Western night club in St. Petersburg's city center. The complex has three bars serving a variety of Western drinks, a dance floor pumping out the latest hip tracks, and a small casino as well. Security is very tight and they have a private taxi service for their guests' convenience. *Quite lively on weekends. Kanal Griboyedova 28. Metro: Nevsky Prospekt. Open 22:00-05:00 daily. Hard currency or rubles. Women are admitted free of charge, men pay an entry fee.*

Tunnel Tucked away on a small side street is this bomb shelter-turned-club where an almost exclusively Russian crowd gyrates away the wee hours to technohouse music. Admission and drinks are cheap, the crowd young, the music ultra-loud and the action continues all through the night. *No street address as it's a bomb shelter. Located on Lyubansky Pereulok in between Ulitsa Blokhina and Zverinskaya Ulitsa. Metro: Gorkovskaya. Open Thur and Sat from midnight until whenever everyone leaves.*

Stardust Located in the Planetarium, this French-British-Russian joint venture has a large restaurant hall with a big stage for performances by actors, singers, dancers, mystics and strippers. A second hall features a technohouse dance club with laser show and between songs they auction all sorts of bizarre items. *Park Lenina 4. Metro: Gorkovskaya. Open 23:00-05:00 Fri and Sat.*

Relax Pop and techno music on a large modern dance floor with video screen, lights, etc. *Prospekt Prosveshcheniya 80. Metro: Grazhdansky Prospekt. Open 22:00-06:00 Fri and Sat.*

Live Music
Rock Around the Clock This exclusive club located in the "Saturn" movie theater features live rock bands in a small club atmosphere. There is a cover charge and the food and drink aren't particularly cheap but the music is usually good and the crowd in a festive mood. *Sadovaya Ulitsa 27. Metro: Sennaya Ploshchad.*

TaMtaM Club offers a genuine peek into the Russian rock and punk scene. Everyone is friends at this small, seedy and somewhat soiled nightspot, and even the cops aren't above joining the fun. Downstairs, cheap and decent snack food and Russian beer is sold. Very cheap and very fun, though it is said that TaMtaM's days are numbered as its owners plan on turning it into a goon cafe. *Corner of Maly Prospekt and 16th Liniya, Vasilievsky Island. Metro: Vasileostrovskaya. Open 19:00-23:00 Fri-Sat.*

Indie Club, located halfway to Siberia, has live music and a bar. Check advertisements to see who is playing, if anyone, as shows are irregular. A little less informal than TaMtaM. *Prospekt Obukhovskoi Oborony 223, inside the Dvorets Kultury Lenina. Metro: Proletarskaya.*

Rock Club The first official rock club in St. Petersburg, this converted palace is host to live music concerts that attract the best local bands as well as groups on tour from other parts of Russia. There is a buffet where you can get snacks and drinks. Performances are irregular so check posters to see if anything is happening. Getting tickets can be a problem and popular shows always sell out - best to go there or to a ticket booth early and try to score. *Ulitsa Rubinshteina 13. Metro: Vladimirskaya/ Dostoevskaya. Tel: 312 3483.*

The Jazz Philharmonic Hall There are two house bands, one a dixieland ensemble and the other a straight-ahead group led by the loquacious co-founder of the club, David Goloshchokin. Local and visiting ensembles take the stage sometimes, and every now and then there are jam sessions. Drinks are available for rubles and hard currency. No smoking in the performance area. You can pick up a schedule there or call. *Zagorodny Prospekt 27. Metro: Vladimirskaya/Dostoevskaya. Open 20:00 until they close, ticket booth open from 14:00-20:00. Tel: 164 8565.*

Kvadrat This jazz club is open on Mondays for performances. Thursday is "club day" where there may be music or else members just sitting around drinking and arguing. *Ulitsa Pravdy 10. Metro: Vladimirskaya/Dostoevskaya. Open 20:00-23:00 Mon and Thur. Tel: 164 5683.*

Bars

The Beer Stube is an Austrian beer hall located in the Nevskij Palace Arcade which offers imported beers and other drinks as well as Austrian snacks and specialities. *Nevsky Prospekt 57. Metro: Mayakovskaya. Open 11:00-24:00. Hard currency, major credit cards accepted. Tel: 275 2001.*

The Beer Garden What better way can there be to enjoy the white nights than to sit in a Western-style beer garden and have a couple of brews? Located in the courtyard behind the Aphrodite restaurant, the Beer Garden serves relatively cheap imported beer and a variety of snacks and is a great place to begin or end an evening. *Nevsky Prospekt 86. Metro: Mayakovskaya. Open 14:00-02:00 May-Sept. Hard currency only. Tel: 275 7620.*

White Nights Bar An open-air bar on the fifth floor of the Hotel Olympia, with live jazz and moderately priced drinks and snacks. Shuttle service to and from the Olympia can be arranged at the concierge desks of either the Olympia or the Grand Hotel Europe. *Ploshchad Morskoi Slavy. Open 15:00-03:00 May-Sept. Hard currency, major credit cards accepted. Tel: 119 6800, 119 6805.*

John Bull Pub It looks and smells like a British pub, and the beer (Skol and John Bull Bitter) is most definitely real. They serve mixed drinks and pub snacks as well. *Nevsky Prospekt 79. Metro: Mayakovskaya. Open 12:00-02:00. Tel: 164 9877.*

Warsteiner Forum A German bar and restaurant with real Bavarian *weiss* beer. Located across from the Moscow Train Station. *Nevsky Prospekt 120. Metro: Ploshchad Vosstaniya. Hard currency only. Open 11:00-02:00. Tel: 277 2914.*

Chaika German pub and food. *Kanal Griboyedova 14. Metro: Nevsky Prospekt. Hard currency only. Open "dayly" 12:00 - 03:00. Tel: 312 4631.*

House Parties
Distant cousins to London's old "acid house" parties, house parties usually take place in a large hall or converted theater and are advertised in Russian on small posters, by word of mouth and on the radio. If you can catch one they're something to experience; huge rooms packed with sound equipment, laser and light shows, and hundreds (sometimes thousands) of young, affluent Russians along with a smattering of foreign students and young business people who dance, drink and party until dawn. Entrance fees to these parties are usually high for Russians and foreigners alike.

Gambling
A big *nyet* throughout the Socialist epoch, gambling has taken St. Petersburg by storm. Slot machines are absolutely everywhere and a number of small casinos with standard offerings (mostly blackjack and roulette) have appeared, with more undoubtedly on the way. The clientele is overwhelmingly Russian, even in hard currency casinos, and slowly and haphazardly people are becoming accustomed to the rules and practices of gambling (though a frightening number of people still split tens).

Needless to say not everyone who hangs out in casinos is a savory character. Some of the smaller casinos can be downright dangerous, particularly if you're a foreigner who has just won a lot of money. Nothing will happen to you inside, but once you step out you may find there are plenty of people interested in sharing your good fortune. We have listed only those casinos we consider reliable and which exhibit high standards of professionalism and guest security.

Conti A small entry fee will get you into this elegant yet unpretentious casino, the largest in St. Petersburg. Clients can relax at the bar, dine at the fine restaurant, watch the show or try their luck at blackjack, poker, roulette and the slot ma-

CASINO CONTI

Welcomes you to the largest casino in St. Petersburg!

Blackjack
Poker
Roulette

Bar & Restaurant
Currency Exchange

Kondratevsky Prospekt 44   Evening dress required

Open from 8pm until 8am

chines. There is a guarded parking lot out front. *Kondratevsky Prospekt 44. Metro: Finlandsky Vokzal then trolleys 3, 12, 19, 38 or 43. Open 20:00-08:00. Rubles only, currency exchange located on premises. Tel: 540 8130.*

Admiral Located in the Hotel Astoria, this small hard currency casino has blackjack, roulette, and slot machines. Evening wear required. *Entry from Ulitsa Gogolya. Open 20:00-06:00. Hard currency only. Tel: 210 5017.*

Palace Casino A British-Russian joint venture casino located in the Music Hall building. Their bar has the cheapest hard currency drinks in the city. *Park Lenina 4. Metro: Gorkovskaya. Open 16:00-04:00. Hard currency and rubles. Tel: 233 9634.*

Argo Not too far from the Sea Terminal on Vasilievsky Island, Argo is a small and comfortable casino with one roulette and four blackjack tables. There is also a bar with drinks and light snacks. *Gavanskaya Ulitsa 2. Metro: Vasileostrovskaya then tram 11, 18 or 40. Open 20:00-08:00. Rubles only. Tel: 217 3409.*

SPECIAL TOURS

On the Water
You can take boat tours around the city and hydrofoils to Petrodvorets and Lomonosov between May and October. Boat tours and the so-called "river trams" which cruise the canals can be caught from the docks in front of Senate Square, by the Hermitage or on the Fontanka River just north of the Anichkov Bridge. Tickets for hydrofoils and cruise boats are sold on a first come, first served basis. Sometimes private owners of boats can be convinced (for a not entirely reasonable sum of cash) to take you for a spin.

In the Air
The more aerially inclined can enjoy some airborne sightseeing by helicopter or light aircraft. This is slightly less spontaneous than boat tours, as companies require reservations at least one day in advance.

The Gatchina Aviation-Sport Club "Dosaaf" offers air tours in small Vilga-35a aircraft and Mi-2 helicopters as well as parachuting, hang gliding and flying lessons. They can issue pilot's licenses, though they are valid only for Russian planes which may not be too useful in countries where you don't have to pedal to keep the propellers going (but they do make great souvenirs). *Tel. in St. Petersburg: 394 3373; in Gatchina: (271) 22 037, (271) 38 101, (271) 61 582.*

Kustanay Air services the entire northwest region of Russia and the Baltic countries with 20-seat Mi-8 passenger helicopters. A wide range of excursion flights covering Pushkin, Petrodvorets and Pavlovsk as well as flights around the city of St. Petersburg are available. *24 hour customer service tel: 465 8810, 465 6161.*

Terminal can fly you around the city in their Mi-8 helicopters or take you to Kizhi, Valaam and the Solovetskiye Islands as well as any other place in the northwest region. Reserve at least two days in advance. *Tel: 311 3725.*

On Horsies
In warmer months you can find kids leading skinny, sad-looking horses around Palace Square and Kazansky Cathedral that are available for short-distance riding. Price needs to be negotiated and they won't let you go too far if they can help it. For more serious riding you'll need to head out to **Olgino** where all year round you can ride for a few dollars per hour. *Telephone in advance for reservations: 238 3132.*

FOR THE BODY

Bath Houses
A trip to the Russian baths (*banya*) can be a memorable experience, but then again so can being stampeded by goats. The *banya* begins in the dressing and undressing room, where everyone strips down (public *banyas* are segregated by sex). Towels in the form of large white sheets are available and most people grab one or two. Warm up in the Finnish-style dry **sauna** (heated to between 100° and 120°C). Take a small break to cool down and then check out the **steam room** (*parilka*), where you can be beaten about the body with dried branches (*vennik*), usually birch, oak or juniper. Half the people in the *parilka* will claim there's not enough heat and start calling for someone to throw more water on the hot rocks, while the other half feebly croak "too much, too much" - the guys who want more steam usually win. This combination of heat, steam and physical abuse purges your body of impurities and gives you a clean unattainable by mere showers or baths.

Once you have been purged to your satisfaction or to the limits of your tolerance, head to the **icy cold pool** (*bassein*) and jump in. Assuming you survive this, you should head back to the steam room or stand under a warm shower so you don't catch cold. Repeat the cycle one or two more times and then stagger back to the dressing room for some tea (people usually bring their own in thermoses). Those with more masochistic instincts will drink beer or vodka, though be warned that the dehydration will make you get drunk fast and these places are mighty slippery. Serious *banya* patrons stay for about three hours. Don't bring too much money as your wallet will be left practically unattended in the dressing room while you are cooking. *Fresh tip*: If you have a history of heart trouble do not do any of this, unless you want to spend your last hours on earth in a room filled with sweaty, naked people.

Some Banyas

Larger *banyas* can accommodate men and women on the same day (on different floors, of course - men go to the мужское отделение and women to the женское отделение), though smaller ones have alternating days for each of the sexes. Try to find the best class (called either люкс or высший класс). It is best to either call in advance (needless to say, nobody will speak any English) or to go with someone who has been before and can sort everything out. Private dressing rooms can be rented for a little extra, or in evenings hire the entire *banya* for a private party.

Nevsky Banya: *Ulitsa Marata 5/7. Metro: Mayakovskaya. Tel: 312 1379.*

Banya #50: *Malaya Posadskaya 28. Metro: Gorkovskaya. Tel: 233 5092.*

Banya #13 has a huge outdoor heated swimming pool for co-ed plunging. It's really cool in the winter when it's snowing. *Karbysheva Ulitsa 29a. Metro: Ploshchad Muzhestva. Tel: 550 0985.*

Banya #9 has an excellent and exclusive luxury-class set-up on the top floor. *Ulitsa Degtyarnaya 1-a. Metro: Ploshchad Vosstaniya. Tel: 274 5621.*

Working Out

World Class Gym has small and pricey fitness centers in the Grand Hotel Europe and the Astoria which include solariums, saunas, some weight machines and jacuzzis. They also have a larger complex in town with a work-out room, excercycles and stair machines, an aerobics room, a solarium and massage parlor. *Kamennostrovsky Prospekt 26/28. Metro: Gorkovskaya. Open 09:00-22:00 Mon-Fri, 11:00-21:00 Sat-Sun. Hard currency for foreigners. Tel: 232 7581.*

For people interested in traditional local work-outs, try the following:

> For your **quads**, run after trolleybuses (experts should try this on Nevsky Prospekt during rush hour, loaded down with large shopping bags). Alternatively, run up the down escalator in the metro.
>
> For **biceps**, try lifting shots of vodka slowly from the table to your lips and back down again. After ten repetitions your biceps should be numb.
>
> To tone your **stomach**, drink some tap water and wait four to six weeks.
>
> You can combine a full body **massage** with a quick **sauna** by riding the metro in the summer during peak hours, though beating fellow passengers with birch branches is not advised.

FOR THE SOUL

Russians have always been a spiritual people, and religion has returned with a vengeance from the dog days of State sponsored and enforced atheism. **Russian Orthodoxy** remains the most prominent faith here, but the spiritual vacuum left by Communism has attracted fringe religions from all around the globe, like Hare Krishnas (who parade down Nevsky Prospekt and hold informal jam sessions), Jehovah's Witnesses (who bombard passersby with leaflets and American accents), Moonies (who brainwash young kids by taking them on retreats, underfeeding them and making them sing "We are the World" over and over) and Mormons (clean cut college boys with white teeth and nice suits who insist on being called "Elder").

Russian Orthodox services are held two or three times daily. People get pretty into it, standing through the entire liturgy, bowing, chanting and singing, so if you go during a service be respectful and dress appropriately. Women are required to cover their heads before entering a church.

Places of Worship

Russian Orthodox:

Holy Trinity Cathedral (*Svyatotroitsky Sobor*). In the Alexander Nevsky Monastery. *Metro: Ploshchad Alexandra Nevskogo. Tel: 274 0409.*

St. Nicholas' Cathedral (*Nikolsko-Bogoyavlensky Sobor*): Located in a beautiful part of town where Kanal Griboyedova and the Kryukov Kanal meet. *Nikolskaya Ploshchad 1/3. Metro: Sadovaya then two tram stops or a 15 minute walk down Sadovaya Ulitsa. Tel: 114 0862.*

Cathedral of the Transfiguration (*Spaso-Preobrazhensky Sobor*). *Ploshchad Radishcheva 1. Metro: Chernyshevskaya. Tel: 272 3662.*

Church of the Vladimir Icon of Our Lady (*Tserkov vo imya Vladimirskoi ikony Bozhei Materi*): Unlike the previous Cathedrals, this church was left to fall into disrepair by the Communist government and only recently was it returned to the Orthodox Church. It has been partially restored but still has a long way to go. *Vladimirskaya Ploshchad 20. Metro: Vladimirskaya. Tel: 113 1614.*

Other:

Armenian: Church of the Holy Resurrection. *Naberezhnaya Reki Smolenki 29, Vasilievsky Island. Metro: Primorskaya. Tel: 350 5301.*

Buddhist Temple: *Primorsky Prospekt 91. Metro: Chernaya Rechka and a 15 minute walk along the river. Tel: 239 0341.*

Catholic: Church of Our Lady at Lourdes. *Kovensky Pereulok 7. Metro: Ploshchad Vosstaniya. Tel: 272 5002.*

Jewish Synagogue. *Lermontovsky Prospekt 2. No nearby metro. Tel: 114 1153.*

Moslem Mosque. *Kronverksky Prospekt 7. Metro: Gorkovskaya. Tel: 233 9819.*

CRUELTY TO ANIMALS

The St. Petersburg **Circus** will send shivers down the spines of animal lovers. Robotic monkeys, camels and (when they have them) bears do ridiculous stunts before bolting off stage to the safety of their dirty, microscopic cages. If this doesn't turn you off, then you can sit back and enjoy contortionists, acrobats and clowns doing regular circus stuff. The acts are far from extraordinary and the exploitation of tortured animals stretches the boundaries of entertainment. *Naberezhnaya Reki Fontanki 3. Metro: Gostiny Dvor. Tickets available on the premises or in kassas around town. Foreigners must pay in hard currency. Tel: 210 4390.*

A trip to the **St. Petersburg Zoo** makes hunting seem humane. If you're going to kill animals, at least do it quickly and not draw it out in front of a bunch of kids. Don't go unless you want to be really depressed. *Park Lenina 1. Metro: Gorkovskaya. Open daily 10:00-16:00 in winter, until 18:00 in autumn, until 19:00 in spring and until 22:00 in summer.*

SHOPPING

S HOPPING IN RUSSIA has never been easy. "Shop till you drop" takes on a whole new meaning when faced with long lines, empty shelves and the flailing elbows of determined old ladies. If finding basic consumer goods is a full time job for Russians, foreign visitors can expect to be confused, frustrated and eventually exhausted by the sheer inefficiency of it all. The change to a free-market economy has alleviated the situation to some extent by providing a wider variety of imported products as well as a steadily increasing number of well-stocked hard currency and commercial ruble shops, but inadequate distribution networks, the devaluation of the ruble and runaway inflation still conspire to make shopping a challenge.

Demand for many things still exceeds supply so if you see something you think you might possibly want, decide quickly. The sale of prized items is publicized by a frighteningly efficient word-of-mouth system and things go fast. By the time you've thought "that's nice, I'll pick it up tomorrow" it may already be too late. For this reason basic shopping strategy while in St. Petersburg is, "if you see it, grab it; if you need it, hoard it." Whenever you go out take a "just in case" bag with you to accommodate any sudden purchases you might make ("Ohmigod - Cheese!") because shopping bags are not given by most shops (although some do amazing wrapping jobs with brown paper and string).

Visitors will find a growing number of what are considered luxury shops stocking imported wares with price tags displaying dollar signs or ruble figures with numerous zeros. Western products are unaffordable to all but a small percentage of the population, so many of these new stores are more like museums. *And in aisle seven, we have the history of toothpaste exhibit.*

Although the **opening hours** of shops vary, most open at 09:00 or 10:00 and close between 18:00 and 20:00, Monday to Saturday, with a one hour lunch break from 13:00 to 14:00 or 14:00 to 15:00. The best time to venture out is undoubtedly morning when deliveries are made and before the ravenous hoards hit the streets. Try to avoid the shopping rush hours between 15:00 and 18:00 when crowds can be particularly vicious.

Where to Shop
Trying to find a shop that sells what you want to buy can sometimes be an arduous task. In the old days things were significantly simpler: stores were named after the item that hopefully existed at the end of a very long line. You could wait in line for cheese at the сыр store, wait in line for meat at the мясо store, wait in line for drinks at the вино — водка store or wait in line for everything at the универсам or not-so-supermarket. These days things have become so confusing that you can wait in line for shoes at the carpet store or buy a Mercedes Benz at the flower shop without waiting in line at all. Nevertheless most stores, particularly those that sell food, are still called by the old system of naming a store after their main item, (фрукты — овощи, молоко, etc.).

Many stores continue to operate on the old system of payment, which was designed by the Marquis de Sade. Intended to both relieve any single person of the responsibility of making a sale and to create jobs, the system requires that you stand in one line to pay for an item and another line to pick it up. You may have already stood in a line just to get to a position where you can see what's for sale and how much it costs, and for food items bought by weight, it must be weighed first (for which you will need to wait in line). For most larger items like books, clothes and "expensive" (in the ruble sense of the word) goods, the person working at the particular department (отдел) will need to write you a check which you take to the cashier. Non-Russian speakers can have a hard time with this system;

pointing, pantomime and waving money around should get the message across but positive results depend on the mood of the extremely underpaid and bored staff. Questions like "Do you have this in black?" are likely to be ignored - usually what you see is what there is. Queue to pay at the KACCA (cashier). You will need to communicate to the cashier how much the item(s) you want to buy costs and possibly from which department. After paying you will be handed a receipt which you trade for the goods back at the отдел (after queuing one last time).

Magazin-Salons
The first dose of privatization and entrepreneurialism has caused a rash of commercial shops to break out all over town. Perhaps it is homage to the old Soviet days of uniformity that they are practically all called *Magazin-Salon* (магазин — салон) and have similar inventories: cheap clothes from China, bootleg jeans and shoes, imported cosmetics, Third World chocolates, blue liqueurs and a smattering of imported electronic goods and stereo equipment (some of which still even have serial numbers). These stores cater mostly to the younger generation of hipsters, yuppies and wheeler-dealers and the service is usually (though not always) less surly than State stores and the crowds smaller. Goods turn over fast with a new but remarkably similar inventory every week or two. Within the *magazin-salon* circuit are some specialized stores that sell (in addition to the standard wares listed above) imported toilets and car parts or other items in hot demand. There are also *magazin-salons* that call themselves Commercial Shops, or Коммерческий магазин. A lot of these stores boast signs that say "Tax Free" or "Duty Free" though these claims have no relation at all to reality. The payment system in these private shops is either by the old inconvenient KACCA system or by the more modern approach of paying the person who hands you the goods.

Kiosks

Convenience shopping has finally hit St. Petersburg. The free market manifests itself at street-level in kiosks as well as on portable stands, folding tables and off the backs of trucks. Kiosk cities have sprung up near every metro station and just about anywhere else where people might pass or where there is sufficient sidewalk space. Hours vary and depend on what is sold in the kiosk, the area of town and how much protection money is paid. In general, kiosks resemble *magazin-salons* in small ugly boxes and they are convenient for buying cigarettes, sweets and drinks, though be wary of vodka and cognac - kiosks are infamous dumping grounds for bottled filth (see *Food and Drink*). There are also kiosks specializing in clothes, bootleg tapes, transport tickets, newspapers, books, theater tickets and produce.

Shopping for Food and Drink

St. Petersburg, like Western cities, has plenty of shops where one can find everything necessary to prepare a meal - provided you are on a potato-only diet. More complex diets will inevitably require more work. Going from shop to shop and buying one item at a time is a task better left to people with large amounts of time on their hands. The *universam*, *gastronom* and *produkty* shops combine food groups, so it is possible to kill two or three birds with one stone. It should be said that all of the abovementioned places are inconsistent in wares and the quality tends to leave much to be desired.

Bread is available throughout the city at bakeries (булочная). The whites are fairly standard, whereas the famous Russian black bread comes in gradations of darkness, sourness and the heaviness with which it sits in your stomach. It could be said that there is a cult of bread in Russia; not only is it eaten at every meal and drinking bout, but wheat brandishing, broad-jawed peasants are part of standard Socialist imagery, appearing in metro stations, old posters, paintings and mosaics all over the country. Subsidies have kept bread artificially dirt cheap and even in this era of subsidy-busting, bread prices remain very low.

Some popular bakeries (in addition to the hundreds of others around town).

Karavai Bakery Known as "the Scottish Bakery", Karavai is a Scottish-Russian joint venture with nice buns located across from the Tauride Gardens. *Tavricheskaya Ulitsa 33. Metro: Chernyshevskaya then trolley 15 or 18. Open 08:00-20:00 (14:00-15:00).*

Dr. Oetker sells a variety of bread and pastries, as well as imported ice cream and cakes. Long lines. *Nevsky Prospekt 27. Metro: Nevsky Prospekt. Open 08:00-19:00 (13:00-14:00).*

Bahlsen Bakery Bread and Bahlsen products for rubles. *Nevsky Prospekt 142. Metro: Ploshchad Vosstaniya. Open 08:00-20:00 (14:00-15:00) Mon-Sat, until 19:00 Sun.*

Sever Once this was the most famous cake store in the city for its ultra-sweet creations; now they are still in the process of recovering after a period of staple shortages when they could not produce their famous cream. *Nevsky Prospekt 44. Metro: Nevsky Prospekt. Open 10:00-19:00 (13:00-14:00).*

The Astoria Hotel sells cakes and pastries for rubles at a little stand near the Osvam hard currency shop (entry from *Ulitsa Gertsena*). *Open 12:00-19:00.*

Farmers' Markets
The best places to buy **fresh produce** are the farmers' markets, or *rynoks* (рынок). There are eleven of these scattered around town, though the Kuznechny market located by the Vladimirskaya Metro is by far the best. The produce at the markets is of a much higher quality; the meat is fresh, the

vegetables large and healthy looking. There are out-of-season fruits brought up from the southern and eastern republics, herbs and greens are available year-round; honey, nuts, pickled everything, smoked meats, flowers, dairy products and other goods are available as well. *And there are no lines.* The reason being, of course, that the prices are outrageously high for the majority of people, making the *rynoks* a haven for the local elite and foreigners. As the *rynoks* cater to a wealthier clientele, they also provide a venue for budding entrepreneurs, such as the pensioners standing near the entrances conveniently selling plastic bags, street vendors, musicians and purveyors of things long stored in closets. There are also pickpockets, so watch your valuables.

Because this is a farmers' market, you have the option of trying something before buying it. Don't be alarmed by the dark hairy guys waving knives at you (provided they are behind the stalls), they just want to offer you a slice of fruit. Feel free to pick a grape before buying, try a forkfull of pickled cabbage, or have some steak tartar. *Fresh Warning*: Trying a handful of everything in sight will only agitate the knife-wielding dark hairy guys, and there are a lot more of them than there are of you.

One of the fun parts of the farmers' market is haggling. Not speaking a common language with the vendor of course greatly reduces your position, though many of the sellers know English numbers. The laws of the bazaar apply here - at every step of the way they will try to screw you. Don't hesitate to refuse a squashed tomato or a droopy rose - the vendor will replace it with no questions asked, and remember to bring along jars for honey and sour cream.

Rynoks are open from 08:00-19:00 Mon-Sat, until 16:00 Sun, and close one day a month so they can mop up the blood.

Kuznechny Rynok - The best, also the most expensive. *Kuznechny Pereulok 3. Metro: Vladimirskaya/Dostoevskaya.*

Kondratevsky/Kalininsky Rynok - On weekends there is a large pet market here with purebred puppies, exotic kittens, chickens, rabbits, sometimes even goats and monkeys. By an amazing coincidence there is also a fur market farther back with some killer hats. *Polyustrovsky Prospekt 45. Metro: Ploshchad Lenina then any bus or trolley which goes to the left as you face the Lenin statue, except the #8.*

Torzhkovsky Rynok - One of the better markets in town. *Torzhkovskaya Ulitsa 20. Metro: Chernaya Rechka.*

Nekrasovsky Rynok - Standard farmers' market fare. It's almost impossible to glean that this is one of the major centers of Petersburg's drug trade. *Ulitsa Nekrasova 52. Metro: Chernyshevskaya.*

Vasileostrovsky Rynok - The selection and quality here are not as high as at other markets, but it is one of the cheapest. *Bolshoi Prospekt 16. Metro: Vasileostrovskaya.*

Ruble Food Shops
Recently there have been ruble mini-markets cropping up with fresh produce, alcoholic beverages and packaged food for sale, most of it imported. Prices are relatively high, often being ruble equivalents of standard hard currency prices, though items may still be cheaper than in hard currency stores.

Babylon Super is St. Petersburg's first large ruble supermarket. They have a huge variety of imported goods, including fresh produce, freshly baked bread, household supplies, a pet food section and everything you'd never thought you'd find in one ruble store. *Maly Prospekt (Petrogradskaya Storona) 54/56. Metro: Petrogradskaya. Open 10:00-20:00 Mon-Sat.*

Gastronom #1 is an extravagantly beautiful pre-Revolutionary food shop that has recently returned to its pre-Revolutionary name, Yeliseyevsky's. The Yeliseyevs were a high-flying merchant family that operated food shops in cities throughout the Russian Empire. Lots of fresh meat and fish on the right side, and the left side sells imported food and drink for rubles. *Nevsky Prospect 56. Metro: Gostiny Dvor. Open 09:00-21:00 (13:00-14:00) Mon-Sat.*

Antanta, tucked away on Vasilievsky Island near the Tuchkov Bridge, has fresh produce, meat and dairy products, canned and packaged goods plus a huge selection of imported and fine domestic alcohol. A little on the expensive side but the quality is high and the service excellent. *Volkhovsky Pereulok 5 (on the corner of Tuchkov Pereulok). No close metro, though trams 11, 18, 33 and 40 stop near it on Sredny Prospekt. Open 11:00-21:00.*

Surprise is part of a bar-cafe complex. Imported produce, cheese, alcohol and freshly baked *pirozhki. Nevsky Prospekt 113. Metro: Ploshchad Alexandra Nevskogo. Open 24 hours (except 16:00-17:00).*

Torgovy Dom na Moike has a food department that includes groceries, meat, fish and alcohol plus a bar to get the shoppers drunk. *Naberezhnaya Reki Moiki 59. Metro: Nevsky Prospekt. Open 10:00-20:00 (14:00-15:00).*

Podsolnukh Look for the big sunflower. A large variety of imported food, alcohol and ice cream. *Liteiny Prospekt 32. Metro: Chernyshevskaya. Open 10:00-19:00 (14:00-15:00) Mon-Fri, from 12:00 Sat.*

Alcohol
As you will no doubt notice, alcohol is available everywhere. Kiosks are a good place to buy beer, champagne and imported spirits, and it seems that the majority of stores, regardless of profile, offer some kind of alcohol. Russian beer is sold on the street in front of metros and in kiosks. Due to the proliferation of all sorts of heinous liquids peddled in alcohol bottles, the safest bet when purchasing alcohol is to buy it from a respectable looking commercial store.

Nectar is a cafe and wine-tasting hall that includes an alcohol retailer. A large assortment of the best Soviet wines is available, as well as safe cognacs, imported wines from Eastern and Western Europe, and imported beers and liquors. There is a money changing booth if you are short of rubles. *Malodetskoselsky Prospekt 25/12. Metro: Tekhnologichesky Institut. Open 11:00-21:00 (14:00-15:00).*

Smirnoff sells its famous vodka and Smirnoff paraphernalia for rubles. *Ulitsa Sadovaya 27. Metro: Sennaya Ploshchad. Open 11:00-20:00.*

Schilkin and Dagvino is a German-Russian liquor store and bar. *Nevsky Prospekt 172. Metro: Ploshchad Alexandra Nevskogo. Open 09:00-21:00 (14:00-15:00).*

Department Stores
There are several large *univermags* in St. Petersburg. These huge shopping complexes have a long way to go before they reach the level of Harrod's, though they certainly have improved on the old days when a laughingly finite selection of goods was repeated department after department. Retailers rent stalls and rooms in these huge complexes and the variety of goods is constantly increasing. Some *univermags* are home to hard currency shops as well. Note that since the stalls inside are continually changing, finding a specific item may require some intrepid searching.

Major univermags are open from 10:00 to 21:00 and are closed on Sundays.

Gostiny Dvor is a combination of locally produced goods (from shoes to funky suits, children's toys to cheap jewelry, cutlery to sports equipment) and little commercial shops selling imported goods in the *magazin-salon* genre. There is an exchange office located on the second floor, near the Littlewoods shop. *Nevsky Prospekt 35. Metro: Gostiny Dvor.*

Passazh, across Nevsky from Gostiny Dvor, is a smaller and more elite department store that is worth a visit for its pre-Revolutionary style and its eclectic selection of domestic and imported goods. There is a currency exchange office in the middle of the ground floor. *Nevsky Prospekt 48. Metro: Gostiny Dvor.*

DLT, once a children's department store, now sells all sorts of goods for rubles and hard currency but still has an extensive toy department. *Bolshaya Konyushennaya 21/23. Metro: Nevsky Prospekt. Open 10:00-20:00.*

Apraksin Dvor is run-down and creepy. On the perimeter there are a lot of new *magazin-salon* type stores, and the courtyard is home to an ultra-crowded open-air bazaar. *Mafiosi* types stand by the entrances and take a small entry fee. All kinds of everything (most of it junk) can be found here, though keep an eye on your valuables because professional sharpers lurk the premises and if you look foreign you are asking for unwanted attention. *Sadovaya Ulitsa across from Gostiny Dvor. Metro: Gostiny Dvor.*

Moskovsky Department Store occupies two long buildings on opposite sides of Moskovsky Prospekt. Not quite as classy as DLT or Passazh. *Moskovsky Prospekt 205 and 220. Metro: Moskovskaya.*

Books and Posters
Alas the days of English-language propaganda, posters adorned with hammers and sickles and dirt cheap coffee-table art and picture books are coming to an end which is taking most of the fun out of book and poster shopping. Still, every now and then a good relic turns up, and art and picture books are high quality and generally cheaper than in the West. There are also some old-book stores, called either *Stariye knigi* (Старая книга) or *Antikvariat* (Антиквариат), which sell old books and prints, and occasionally a real collector's item can be found.

Dom Knigi is the largest bookstore in St. Petersburg and is housed in the pre-Revolutionary Singer Sewing Company building. Once a haven of kitschy posters, miserable propaganda and reams of technical literature, it has become home to computer software and hardware dealers, and there are a few books here as well. Check out the English language section to the left of the main entrance; art books and currency exchange are on the second floor. Cossack soldiers dressed in colorful uniforms and touting long swords provide the security here. Cossacks are becoming increasingly popular for security because they are traditionally more efficient than militiamen and because they're bad-ass dudes. *Nevsky Prospekt 28. Metro: Nevsky Prospekt. Open 10:00-20:00.*

Mir has two bookstores with lots of art books and photo albums. The one at Nevsky 13 has a small selection of used English-language books, and Nevsky 16 has some souvenirs and art. *Nevsky Prospekt 13 and 16. Metro: Nevsky Prospekt. Open 10:00-19:00 (14:00-15:00) Mon-Sat.*

Bukinist has a good collection of old books and prints. *Liteiny Prospekt 59. Metro: Mayakovskaya. Open 10:00-18:00 (14:00-15:00). Next door is Na Liteinom, a similar antiquarian store with the same hours.*

Cassettes, Records and CDs

Bootleg cassettes of Russian and Western music can be purchased all over town in specialized stores and in select kiosks around metro stations. These kiosks are labeled Звукозапись and usually list Western groups in English. The tapes themselves are mostly of miserable quality and the recording quality varies from heinous to passable. For a larger selection of unlicensed pop, rock, house, disco and jazz recordings, stores and kiosks are springing up that make tapes from their master collections of CDs and albums. In these stores indexed catalogues of albums (in English) hang on the walls; write down the number of what you want and give it to the cashier.

They'll copy the album from CD to cassette in about a week (they have various types there or you can bring your own). The quality is usually pretty good and the price is quite low, so if you don't have any moral aversion to ripping money out of Sting's pocket this is a great way to expand your music collection.

There are considerably fewer **records and CD**'s floating around the city. Most locally produced CD's are classical, and the selection of records tends to be eclectic - lots of classical, a couple of token jazz records, Russian rock and folk music and some big-name Western artists (Bob Marley, Rolling Stones, etc.). It's almost worth the few cents to have an album with your favorite star's name transliterated into Russian. Record stands are in all the *univermags* and in the following stores:

Garmonia The oldest of the bootleg tape stores. Large selection of music and large crowds. *Shpalernaya Ulitsa 44a. Metro: Chernyshevskaya. Open 10:00-19:00 Mon-Fri, 13:00-18:00 Sat.*

Rock Shop The largest collection of Russian music in the city, as well as CDs, cassettes, T-shirts and other rock 'n roll paraphernalia. Totally inconveniently located in the middle of nowhere, but worth the trip for those interested in acquiring some Russian rock records. *Manchesterskaya Ulitsa 10. Metro: Udelnaya. Open 11:00-19:00 Mon-Sat.*

Rock Island, near the Spartak movie theater, is like Rock Shop, only the assortment is smaller. *Ulitsa Saltykova-Shchedrina 10. Metro: Chernyshevskaya. Open 10:00-20:00 Mon-Sat.*

Melodiya Records, CDs and things vaguely related to them (TVs, phones etc.). *Nevsky Prospekt 32/34. Metro: Nevsky Prospekt. Open 11:00-19:00 (14:00-15:00) Mon-Sat.*

Photographic Supplies, Film and Developing, Passport Photos
Agfa sells and develops film and has a small supply of cameras and photo equipment. They also do xeroxing and passport photos. *Nevsky Prospekt 20. Metro: Nevsky Prospekt. Open 10:00-20:00. Hard currency only.*

Kodak Express has several one-hour color film developing places that sell film and photo equipment and do xeroxing and passport photos. *Malaya Konyushennaya 7 (Metro: Nevsky Prospekt); Open 09:00-21:00 daily. Ulitsa Gertsena 32 (Metro: Nevsky Prospekt); Open 09:00-20:00 daily. Nevsky Prospekt 103 (Metro: Ploshchad Vosstaniya); Open 10:00-19:00 Mon-Sat.*

Fuji sells and develops film, and has a small supply of equipment as well. They do passport photos and can develop E-6 slides. *Naberezhnaya Reki Fontanki 23. Metro: Gostiny Dvor. Open 10:00-21:00 Mon-Sat.*

Liteiny 23 has while-u-wait passport photos and also does portraits. *Liteiny Prospekt 43. Metro: Mayakovskaya. Walk through the labyrinth of courtyards following the FOTO signs till you find it. Open 11:00-19:30 (14:00-15:00) Mon-Fri.*

Art and Souvenirs
Finding souvenirs in St. Petersburg is never a problem. If you are on any kind of tour or hanging around a tourist sight looking foreign, they will find you, in the form of dolls (*matryoshkas*), fur hats, cans of caviar and other assorted junk thrust in your face by pimply teenagers. If the monotony of this does not diminish your desire to pick up a little something as a gift or memento, then there are several stores and galleries that would be more than happy to accommodate your needs. You can find standard souvenir items in all the major department stores mentioned above. In addition there is a souvenir bazaar in between *Inzhenernaya Ulitsa* and *Manezhnaya Ploshchad* called *Klenovaya Alleya* (or Maple Lane in English) where young scruffy types hawk standard souvenir stuff. Haggle, or they'll take you to the cleaners.

Street Art

Nevsky is lined with artists and art dealers displaying their wares. Almost all the stuff is souvenir quality or worse and prices generally correspond to this. For higher quality artwork, check out some of the galleries dotting the city. Generally the ones concentrated around Nevsky and other touristy locations have more kitschy stuff in them.

Recommended Galleries

Palitra Whereas most of the galleries on Nevsky are havens of uninteresting kitsch, Palitra is a serious gallery for people seriously interested in art. Works by respected Petersburg artists are exhibited here, and the artists themselves hang out on occasion for a cup of coffee at the gallery's cafe. An English-speaking guide/art critic will be happy to show you around. This is a great place to get acquainted with contemporary Petersburg art. *Nevsky Prospekt 166, enter from courtyard. Metro: Ploshchad Alexandra Nevskogo. Open 11:00-19:00 Tues-Sat. Tel: 277 1216.*

Anna Gallery This modern-art gallery exhibits and sells works by the most skillful and talented artists of Russia and the former Republics. An English speaking guide can show you around, and full customs support is provided for buyers. *Nevskij Palace Arcade, Nevsky Prospekt 57. Metro: Mayakovskaya. Open 09:00-20:00.*

Petropol exhibits and sells mammoth tusks carved by the best-known mammoth tusk carvers of Russia. They also have catalogues and art books. *Millionnaya Ulitsa 27. Metro: Nevsky Prospekt. Open 10:00-18:00 Tues-Sun. Tel: 315 3414.*

Golubaya Gostinaya (Blue Drawing Room) Located in the Union of Artists' building, the works here are usually less interesting than the other temporary exhibits located elsewhere in the building. Around the back of the building (entrance from Moika 83) there is a modern art gallery. *Ulitsa Gertsena 38. Metro: Nevsky Prospekt. Tel: 315 7414, 314 4734.*

Pushkinskaya 10/10 Located in a building that has been at the center of Petersburg's hip art scene for the last several years, this gallery features works of interesting local artists. *Pushkinskaya Ulitsa 10, apt. 10, on the 3rd floor. Metro: Mayakovskaya. Open 12:00-19:00 Mon-Sat. Tel: 315 2832.*

Laundry
Petersburg is pretty bad news in this department. Though some hotels offer laundry and dry-cleaning services for their guests, they are generally too overloaded to take in clothes from non-guests. You can risk having things dry-cleaned at any *khimchistka* (химчистка) around town though these places are renowned for losing buttons, ruining special-care materials and occasionally losing Armani suits that happen to fit one of the workers.

Hair Care
There are people ever ready and willing to cut hair in most hotels, and if the hotel is a major tourist haven it is most likely that the scissors-wielder will speak some English. Anyone looking for a little more adventure can take their chances at a random hairdresser's (парикмахерская); here you can expect no foreign language ability and who knows what will happen to your head.

Wella Salon Debut recreates the atmosphere of a London High Street or West Hollywood salon, right down to the chi-chi bearded guys in white jumpsuits. The staff is Western trained, use Western products and charge Western prices. Also hair care products for sale. *Nevsky Prospekt 54. Metro: Gostiny Dvor. Hard currency only. Open 09:00-20:00 Mon-Sat. Tel: 312 3026.*

Ciao has a hair salon in the back of a pricey hard currency shop that sells women's clothing, lingerie, makeup and $10 tupperware containers. The hair staff is Italian trained and haircuts are relatively cheap. Prices of haircuts are in rubles, although extremely complicated ones that involve the use of many Western materials are charged in hard currency (payable in rubles according to their rate). *Naberezhnaya Reki Fontanka 5. Metro: Gostiny Dvor and a 15 minute walk. Open 10:00-19:00 (13:00-14:00) Mon-Sat. Tel: 314 0080.*

Hard Currency Stores

Hard currency stores in St. Petersburg are mostly mini-markets that stock a small variety but broad cross-section of goods, including booze, sweets, food, clothes, electronics and homewares. Though many of the items can be found for rubles around town, these stores are convenient as they always stock high-quality goods and they can save you the hassle of running around looking in various shops for whatever you need.

Spar Market is St. Petersburg's first large hard currency supermarket. The vast food section features high quality meats, dairy products and an array of fruits and vegetables that will knock a vegetarian's socks off. There is also a large selection of alcoholic beverages, a pharmaceutical counter and even a car parts section. A currency exchange booth is located on the premises. *Prospekt Slavy 30. Metro: Moskovskaya then trolleys 27 or 29, or Lomonosovskaya then trolley 27. Open 10:00-20:00. Major credit cards accepted. Tel: 260 4121. Also on Prospekt Stachek 1. Metro: Narvskaya. Tel: 186 9411.*

Express Market features a wide selection of imported food and drink with everything from fresh produce to canned and frozen goods. They also have lots of household items, alcohol and foreign-language newspapers and journals. *Moskovsky Prospekt 73. Metro: Frunzenskaya. Tel: 252 4144. Also Ulitsa Kharkovskaya 1. Metro: Ploshchad Vosstaniya. Tel: 277 7771. Both markets open 10:00-20:00. Major credit cards and travellers cheques accepted.*

Stockmann's has a large selection of food, including fresh dairy products, meat, fish and bread, and some homewares as well. *Finlandsky Prospekt 1. Metro: Ploshchad Lenina. Open 10:00-20:00. Major credit cards accepted. Tel: 542 2297, 542 3676.*

The Neva Star, located in the lobby of the Hotel Moskva, sells a variety of food and alcohol as well as Levis jeans, suits, leather jackets, stereo equipment and cosmetics. Prices are at normal European levels though they do have sales every now and then. In the Pribaltiskaya Hotel is the **Baltic Star** which sells a larger array of like goods. *Both stores open daily 08:00-23:00. Major credit cards and travellers cheques accepted. Neva Star tel: 274 0012; Baltic Star tel: 356 4185.*

The International Shop inside the Astoria Hotel offers standard hard currency shop wares. *Entrance from Ulitsa Gogolya. Open daily 09:00-21:00. Major credit cards and travellers cheques accepted.*

Also on the other side of the Astoria is **Osvan**, a new Swedish-Russian joint venture selling watches, shoes and the usual assortment of booze, sweets, etc. *Entrance from Ulitsa Gertsena. Open daily 10:00-22:00.*

Viking, in the Hotel St. Petersburg, has a reasonable selection of food (no fresh produce), alcohol, sweets, coffee, tea, spices and condiments. *Vyborgskaya Naberezhnaya 5. Metro: Ploshchad Lenina. Open daily 10:00-20:00 (13:00-14:00). Tel: 542 8709.*

Home Center has everything needed for settling in. Appliances, cleaning materials, hardware and other hard to find home improvement items are on hand. *Prospekt Slavy 30/2. Metro: Moskovskaya then trolleys 27 or 29, Metro: Lomonosovskaya then trolley 27. Open 10:00-20:00. Major credit cards accepted. Tel: 260 7224.*

COMMUNICATING WITH THE OUTSIDE WORLD

IF YOU COUNT ON STATE-RUN services, communication with the outside world can be somewhat hampered. Mail from Russia typically takes over a month to reach any destination and the telephone system, though cheaper than their Western equivalents, is still rather primitive. If a phone call or package just has to get through, these services present a considerable risk. Fortunately there exist a number of alternatives to standard State service, which are naturally more expensive but also much more reliable.

TELEPHONE AND FAX

Russia's country code is 7
St. Petersburg's city code is 812
Moscow's city code is 095

State Service
International phone service took a great leap forward in April 1993 when a phone cable from Moscow and St. Petersburg to Copenhagen was put into operation. At long last people in these cities can dial directly to just about any place on the planet, with the exception of locations in the former Soviet Union which are still mostly serviced by the old styrofoam cup and string system. Traffic is rather heavy on this new line, so don't be surprised if you don't get through the first few times. To call from a private telephone or hotel **dial 8** and wait for the second dial tone, then dial 10, the desired country code, city code and phone number. You'll need to be patient and persistent; be prepared to put some time into dialing and redialing and redialing...

If you cannot get through at all, you can call the international operators at **315 0012**. If you don't speak Russian, say "*Ya ne gavaryu po russki*" ("I don't speak Russian") or simply ask for someone who speaks English. They will either hang up on you or fetch an English-speaking operator. Tell the operator what country you want to call, and he or she will tell you the earliest time you can call, which may end up being tomorrow. Pleading, even crying, is unlikely to be met with much success. To make the reservation you need to give the phone number you will be calling from and specify whether it is in a hotel or private flat. Since the lines have so much traffic, these booked calls rarely come through on time. Just sit by the phone and wait; the operator will call you when the call is placed.

Central Telephone Office
Long distance domestic and international calls can be made at the **Central Telephone Office** located between Nevsky Prospekt and the Triumphal Arch that leads to Palace Square. In some cases it would be quicker to fly home and personally deliver the message; expect long waits and be prepared to return the following day if you are trying to call an off-the-beaten-track country like Australia or Zimbabwe. You must pay for the call when you reserve it (calls to the US use window 16, all other countries use window 13). Asking for (or writing down) Express (*srochny* | срочный) may get your call through with less wait for twice the price.

To the immediate left of the entrance there are several phone booths with direct dial to the US, Finland and Eastern European countries. To use these phones you will need to pick up a token (*zheton*) from the person in the booth. Wait in line for your turn and then go to the indicated booth. Dial the number and when the connection is made push the black "answer" (ответ) button on the phone box to establish communication. After the call, return the *zheton* and pay.

The Telephone Office is packed with phone booths that are labelled with specific cities and regions which the phones access, as well as phones that access all cities in the former Soviet Union (marked многозоновый). Buy your *zhetons* from the booth next to the slot machines along the right-hand wall as you enter. Dial 8 to get the inter-city dial tone, then the city code and phone number. Press the ответ button to start talking. These phones eat *zhetons* rather fast, so you may need to buy a lot.

Faxes can be sent and received from here as well. Go to window 15 and fill out the little form (in Russian only), listing the destination country, phone and fax number. Faxes are sent within one to three days, or for double the cost they can be sent within two hours. **The Central Telephone Office's fax receiving number is (+7 812) 315 1701**. They will hold a fax for one month. Call 314 0140 to inquire if anything has come for you. *The Central Telephone Office is at Ulitsa Gertsena 3. Metro: Nevsky Prospekt. Open 08:00-22:00, fax desk from 09:00-21:00.*

Public pay phones are located all over the city, though finding one that hasn't been vandalized can be harder than finding a flying penguin. Coins must be placed in the cradle on top of the phone before dialing; when your call connects the coin will drop. Pay phones are being converted from taking 15 kopeck coins to take metro tokens. If you hear a series of beeps you are just about to be cut off, so put another coin in fast. Inter-City pay phones can be found on some major streets and are marked with a red and blue telephone logo and the word междугородный. The same rules apply to these phones as to those in the Central Telephone Office, including the ответ button on the phone box.

Private Services
There are three alternatives to the State phone system: satellite, cellular or land-line systems.

Baltic Communications Ltd (BCL), a British, American and Russian joint venture, provides international telephone, fax and data services throughout St. Petersburg. Utilizing the most modern digital technology, worldwide service is available from guest rooms and business centers at the Nevskij Palace, Pulkovskaya and St. Petersburg Hotels, as well as the Neptune Hotel/Business Center. BCL also provides a variety of other services including direct dial lines for office or home use and Global Connect Calling Card. The BCL network is entirely independent of the old Soviet-built telephone system, and provides instant, reliable and high-quality connections. *Konnogvardeisky Bulvar 4. Hard currency, rubles and major credit cards accepted. Tel: 314 5548; Fax: 314 8660.*

Peterstar can hook up businesses to a digital network which provides local, national and international voice, fax and data access. They have also installed several credit card phone booths around town that provide their high quality connections for reasonable prices, and the good news is that you don't have to have a credit card as you can pick up a special Peterstar card from the establishment where the phone is located. *Peterstar phone booths are installed around the city, including the Grand Hotel Europe, the John Bull Pub, the Antwerpen Cafe and a number of other convenient locations. Office address: 16th Liniya 31, Vasilievsky Island. Metro: Vasileostrovskaya. Tel: 119 6060; Fax: 119 9002.*

Delta Telecom is well established and currently the only mobile cellular telephone service in St. Petersburg. Delta's time-tested network provides reliable local, inter-city and international connections with sturdy, advanced mobile phones available on a monthly basis. Their phones operate on the 450 MHz Nordic standard. *Ulitsa Gertsena 22. Metro: Nevsky Prospekt. Tel: 315 7513; Fax 314 8837.*

Faxes and telexes can be also sent from business centers of larger hotels at varyingly high prices, and they are sent out immediately.

Mail, Express Mail and Telegrams

The Main Post Office (*Glavpochtamt***)** sells stamps and envelopes (when they have them) and handles international mail (counter 24) and packages (counters 25-27), though don't expect any foreign language support. There are many bizarre restrictions on what you can send out; these change frequently and a lot depends on who you're dealing with. Packages are inspected and wrapped here, though you can bring your own materials if you want, and you must fill out many copies of various customs forms. Packages are sent by continental drift. Addressing **Poste Restante** to Santa Claus, The North Pole, would probably be as effective as using the real address, which is:

190000 St. Petersburg   190000 Санкт Петербург
Glavpochtamt   Главпочтамт
Do vostrebovaniya   До востребования

Pochtamtskaya Ulitsa 9. Metro: Nevsky Prospekt then trolley 5, 14 or 22 to St. Isaac's Square. Open 09:00-20:00 Mon-Sat, 10:00-15:00 Sun.

Smaller post offices (Почта) around the city can do almost everything the Main Post Office does (though they don't take international packages and few bother with international mail). Some offer faxing services. Real risk-lovers can drop mail in the blue mailboxes located all over town.

American Express cardholders can receive mail at the American Express office in the Grand Hotel Europe. Mail should be addressed to:

c/o American Express
P.O. Box 87
SF-53501 Lappeenranta
Finland

DHL began operating in Russia in 1984 (six years before anyone else) and is the recognized leader in the express-mail business in this part of the world. Through their network of over 20 city offices across the CIS they can deliver to any location in the CIS, including overnight to Moscow. They have drop-off points all over town, including a spanking new customer service center in the Nevskij Palace Arcade. Documents, parcels, customs clearance and door-to-door service. *Main drop-off point: Nevsky Prospekt 57; also at the Grand Hotel Europe, the Hotel Olympia and the Hotel Astoria. Open 09:00-18:00 Mon-Fri, call for weekend service. Hard currency or rubles, all credit cards, travellers cheques, bank transfers and any other form of payment accepted. Tel. for pick up: 311 2649, 314 6473, 210 7654, 210 7545; Fax: 314 6473.*

EMS has courier services to Russian and former Soviet locations as well as international air delivery of letters and packages. *Konnogvardeisky Bulvar 4, 1st entry. Branches located in the Moskva and Pribaltiskaya Hotels. Open 09:00-18:00. Tel: 311 9671, 311 1120; Fax 311 9738.*

Telegrams

Telegrams can be sent from the Main Post Office, the Central Telephone Office or from ТЕЛЕГРАФ offices located throughout the city. They're reliable and quite cheap. Fill out a blank international (международная) form (in Latin letters) and pay. Write your name and address on the bottom.

Electronic Mail

Sovam Teleport, a Russian-British-American joint venture, offers complete electronic mail, on-line database and other information and telecommunication resource services. Customers can send faxes and telexes directly from their PC's via E-Mail, at prices lower than standard international tariffs. One time service, temporary and long-term accounts are available. *Nevsky Prospekt 30. Metro: Nevsky Prospekt. Open 09:00-18:00 Mon-Fri. Hard currency and limited ruble services. Tel: 311 8412; Fax: 311 7120.*

MEDICAL

FALLING ILL IN A STRANGE country can take much of the fun out of travelling. Russia is no exception, being far away from Western medicines, a developed and user-friendly medical infrastructure and Mommy. The climate here is rough, to say nothing about the sanitary conditions. Prepare yourself by having a check-up before you come if you plan on being here for any substantial period of time. It's also not a bad idea to be up to date on your inoculations, just in case. Bring any prescription medicines you may need, as it can be a nuisance trying to find them here. Simpler items (vitamins, cold medicines and aspirin) have become pretty readily available in recent times.

Humid summers, wet slushy winters, sudden temperature jumps and cold gulf winds are most conducive to minor colds and bouts of 'flu and because places like museums and public transport are rather crowded, exposure to such minor illnesses is almost unavoidable. Consider it an extension of the Cold War that local invading germs are so eager to tackle Western defense systems.

Stomach problems are also rather common. The most heinous perpetrator of guttural agony is **the water**. The stuff is contaminated with *giardia lamblia*, a nasty little protozoan which will keep you chained to the WC as well as weak and in pain. **Giardia** can take several weeks to incubate, and its symptoms are pretty recognizable - frequent trips to the bathroom, the inability to keep anything down, inhuman sulfuric smells emitting from your body and so on. The good news is that giardia is easily treated with a medicine called *metronidazole* (or brand name *Flagyl*). There's no need to be paranoid of giardia to the point where you take baths in bottled water, but make sure you drink water that has been boiled for at least five minutes or otherwise purified, and it is advisable to brush your teeth with such water. Other stomach problems can result from improperly cooked or spoiled food. Bring some diarrhoea medicine just in case.

Medical Care

The privilege of socialized medical care is accorded to Russian Federation citizens only. Be thankful for this; the level of free medical care here is so atrocious that in many cases it would be better just to drink lots of tea with honey and hope for the best rather than have underpaid quacks stick dirty needles and rusty knives into your body. Paid medical care is better, but still leaves much to be desired. Be aware that medical equipment and supplies are in very short stock here, and hospitals and clinics are forced to re-use things. It is extremely unlikely that needles will be re-used, but it is always a good idea to bring some clean ones with syringes if you are going to a clinic or hospital for any reason. Even the fancier places that claim they are tailored for Western clientele have a hard time giving up their old habits. In the case of a medical emergency it is advisable to leave the country if you have time (air time to Helsinki: one hour). If you must have surgery or have broken bones cast here, it may not be a bad plan to have someone look at you afterwards in Finland or another country where they have a high level of medical care.

Foreigners usually get treated well at Russian hospitals as it would be a tremendous embarrassment if they bumped you off like they do the rest of their patients. Still, to ensure the best possible attention and highest quality medicines and treatments it is advisable to give the doctor a little something as they are all miserably underpaid. In some cases they won't even look at you without some form of advance payment.

American Medical Center Opening in the summer of 1993, the AMC is staffed by Western doctors and offers a full range of medical care including a trauma centre, evacuation co-ordination and co-operation with high quality Russian hospitals. *Naberezhnaya Reki Fontanka 77. Metro: Sennaya Ploshchad. Hard currency, rubles and major credit cards accepted. Open 08:30-18:00 Mon-Fri. Tel: 310 9611.*

Gastello Hospital Surprisingly good care, probably the best place to go in an emergency. They have some English-speakers. *Ulitsa Gastello 20. Metro: Moskovskaya. Hard currency or rubles. Tel: 293 7010, 291 7960 (call for an ambulance).*

Hospital #26 They have English-speakers on staff, and are more than willing to take hard currency from foreign patients. *Ulitsa Kostyushko 2. Metro: Moskovskaya. Hard currency or rubles. Tel: 123 3209.*

Tamigo A Russian-German joint venture dental center. Call in advance to make an appointment; they work 24 hours a day. *10th Sovetskaya Ulitsa 13. Metro: Ploshchad Vosstaniya. Hard currency or rubles. Tel: 274 6480.*

Polyclinic #18 Children's polyclinic. *Ulitsa Kuibysheva 25. Metro: Gorkovskaya. Tel: 238 1652, 233 5114 (English speaking doctor 10:00-17:30).*

Emergency Evacuation
If there is a serious medical emergency and you need to get out of the country fast, **Jetflite Oy** in conjunction with Hospital Mehiläinen can get a flying ambulance over here fast and whisk you to Helsinki for surgery. It's not exactly cheap, but neither is your life. *Jetflite Oy tel: +358 0 822 766; Fax: +358 0 870 3202, 24 hours a day. Hospital Mehiläinen tel: +358 0 431 4364; Fax: +358 0 431 4218.*

Taking Care of the Naughty Bits
Birth control in Russia is nothing less than a complete disaster. Lack of availability is compounded by lack of knowledge and, as an appalling consequence, abortion still ranks as the main form of birth control. People not planning on remaining celibate should bring their own. In addition, passion may not be the only thing that gets inflamed here; one of the end results of a romantic tryst could be the need for a fat dose of penicillin. Claims of "I don't need one" and "I know my body better than you" and orders to "take that off" may seem convincing in the heat of the moment, but "OWWWCH!!!!" can also be most convincing after the fact. If you are going to frolic with the natives during your stay in Petersburg, be firm in your safety concerns and don't take anything for granted.

If you do wind up with some unwanted organism in your erogenous zones, you can turn to the chain of skin-venereal treatment centers, or "**KVD's**" (*Kozhno-venericheskiye Dispansery*, Кожно — венерические диспансеры). There are so-called "anonymous rooms" where for a fee you can get a check-up and, in the event of an unpleasant discovery, the necessary prescription. A KVD is located in each administrative region.

KVD #1 *Nalichnaya Ulitsa 19, Vasilievsky Island. Metro: Primorskaya. Tel: 217 0619.*
KVD #14 *Stremyannanya Ulitsa 4. Metro: Mayakovskaya. Tel: 113 1294.*
KVD #15 *Ulitsa Chaikovskogo 15. Metro: Chernyshevskaya. Tel: 273 5253.*

Pharmacies (Аптека)
Several joint venture pharmacies have opened up to peddle imported wares, and Russian *aptekas* are beginning to stock more Western medicines to go along with the usual array of medicinal herbs and voodoo dolls that they have always sold.

Pharmadon Everything from medicines and vitamins to pregnancy tests and contact lens solution. *Zagorodny Prospekt 21. Metro: Vladimirskaya. Tel: 315 9636. Also on Nevsky Prospekt 5. Metro: Nevsky Prospekt. Tel: 312 7078. Both open 09:00-20:00. Hard currency only.*

Damian International Pharmacy A fair supply of imported medicines. *Moskovsky Prospekt 22. Metro: Tekhnologichesky Institut. Open 09:00-20:00 Mon-Fri, 10:00-18:00 Sat. Hard currency and rubles. Tel: 110 1744.*

Petropharm Drank too much vodka or tap water? Then come here - they have both alka-seltzer and metronidazole. Also other imported pharmaceuticals. *Nevsky Prospekt 22. Metro: Nevsky Prospekt. Tel: 311 3949. Nevksy Prospekt 83. Metro: Ploshchad Vosstaniya. Tel: 277 7966. Both open 09:00-20:00 daily except Sat. Hard currency only.*

Opticians
Vision Express is an American-Russian joint venture selling soft contact lenses (from England and the US) as well as a limited stock of saline, disinfectant and enzyme tablets. *Ulitsa Lomonosova 5. Metro: Gostiny Dvor. Open 10:00-18:00. Hard currency only. Tel: 310 1595.*

Linkon gives eye exams and sells contact lenses of Russian manufacture (though the materials are imported) as well as British extended-wear lenses and colored contacts for travellers seeking a new look. *14th Liniya 97, Vasilievsky Island. Metro: Vasileostrovskaya. Open 10:00-19:00 Mon-Fri, 11:00-17:00 Sat. Tel: 355 8388, 218 4190. English spoken.* Retailing branch offices: *Liteiny Prospekt 39* and *Furshtadstskaya Ulitsa 36.*

Exclusive sells glasses and soft contact lenses with a limited supply of solutions. *Nevsky Prospekt 13. Metro: Nevsky Prospekt. Open 10:00-19:00 Mon-Sat (14:00-15:00), Fri until 18:00. Hard currency and rubles. Tel: 311 5093.*

Folk Medicine

Russians, unlike Westerners, have not been spoiled by conveniently packaged cures for headaches, fevers, itches and other minor ailments, as well as highly developed treatments for more complicated diseases. Though Russian scientists are among the most brilliant in the world they have had to deal with a total lack of supplies and appallingly low levels of funding for practical work. Consequently the field of medicine here is, with a few rare exceptions, several decades behind the West. The further one goes out of the big city, the more the field of medicine resembles the snake-venom and witch chants of auld. Folk medicine is still a Russian institution, and many people who cannot afford expensive Western medicines turn to traditional cures when they are suffering.

While we cannot vouch for any of the following treatments, they have been in practice here for years so who knows - there just may be something to them.

AILMENT	TREATMENT
Sore throat	A. Mix the juice of a lemon with one cup of vodka and one cup of oil. Rinse your throat with it and drink.
	B. Mash an onion into pulp, add a little water until you have onion juice, and gargle. Needless to say, don't do this before a date.
Stuffy nose	Mash several cloves of garlic and put them in a pot of boiling water. Stand over the pot and breathe through your nose for five minutes. This will not only clear your nose but it will keep away vampires and pretty much anyone else until the smell wears off in a couple of days.
Cough	A. Before going to bed have a glass of hot beer.
	B. Grate a radish, add some honey and eat. Drink any resulting radish juice as well.

Fever

A. Just before bed rub vodka or spirit on your chest and feet, put some mustard powder in a pair of woollen socks and put them on. Then drink a mixture of milk, honey, baking soda and vodka and go to sleep.

B. Before going to bed stand naked with your ankles in hot water wearing a woollen hat and drink a large mug of tea with honey, jam and at least 100g of vodka.

Upset stomach

Mix a teaspoon each of salt and pepper with 100g of vodka and drink.

Cancer

Take one teaspoon of lighter fluid and one tablespoon of butter two hours before breakfast daily for two months, then take a break for one month before repeating

Tuberculosis

Mix the following ingredients in a large jar or bucket: Ground aloe, 5-star cognac, melted butter, honey, 10 unbroken eggs, juice of 5 lemons, 1 liter yogurt, 1 teaspoon baking soda. Seal the top and keep at 39°C (102 °F) for 21 days. Take the eggs out, discard the yolks and return the shells and whites to the mixture. Stir and drink one tablespoon before every meal.

Ulcer

20 minutes before breakfast eat two raw egg yolks and drink a 50g shot of spirit.

Radiation

Blueberries and blackberries help purge the organism of radiation, so keep a jar of jam handy at all times in case of nuclear attack.

APPENDIX

Name Changes

Outdated Socialist Version	New Official Name
Ulitsa Anny Ulyanovoi Улица Анны Ульяновой	Polozova Ulitsa Полозова улица
Ulitsa Bratstva Улица Братства	Maly Sampsonievsky Prospekt Малый Сампсониевский проспект
Ulitsa Brodskogo Улица Бродского	Mikhailovskaya Ulitsa Михайловская улица
Ulitsa Voinova Улица Воинова	Shpalernaya Ulitsa Шпалерная улица
Ulitsa Voitika Улица Воитика	Vitebskaya Ulitsa Витебская улица
Prospekt Gaza Проспект Газа	Staro-Petergofsky Prospekt Старо−Петергофский проспект
Ulitsa Dzerzhinskogo Улица Дзержинского	Gorokhovaya Ulitsa Гороховая улица
Ulitsa Zhelyabova Улица Желябова	Bolshaya Konyushennaya Ulitsa Большая Конюшенная улица
Ulitsa Kalyaeva Улица Каляева	Zakharievskaya Ulitsa Захарьевская улица
Prospekt Karla Marxa Проспект Карла Маркса	Bolshoi Sampsonievsky Prospekt Большой Сампсониевский проспект
Kirovsky Prospekt Кировский проспект	Kamennostrovsky Prospekt Каменноостровский проспект
Ploshchad Kommunarov Площадь Коммунаров	Nikolskaya Ploshchad Никольская площадь
Krasnaya Ulitsa Красная улица	Galernaya Ulitsa Галерная улица
Ulitsa Krasnoi Konnitsy Улица Красной Конницы	Kavalergardskaya Ulitsa Кавалергардская улица
Kanal Krushteina Канал Крушштейна	Admiralteisky Kanal Адмиралтейский канал
Prospekt Mayorova Проспект Майорова	Voznesensky Prospekt Вознесенский проспект
Prospekt Maxim Gorkogo Проспект Максима Горького	Kronverksky Prospekt Кронверкский проспект
Ulitsa Marii Ulyanovoi Улица Марии Ульяновой	Grafsky Pereulok Графский переулок
Ploshchad Mira Площадь Мира	Sennaya Ploshchad Сенная площадь
Prospekt N.I. Smirnova Проспект Н.И. Смирнова	Lanskoye Shosse Ланское Шоссе

Prospekt Ogorodnikova
Проспект Огородникова
Ulitsa Olega Koshevogo
Улица Олега Кошевого
Ulitsa Petra Lavrova
Улица Петра Лаврова
Pereulok Podbelskogo
Переулок Подбельского
Bulvar Profsoyuzov
Бульвар Профсоюзов
Ulitsa Rakova
Улица Ракова
Ploshchad Revolutsii
Площадь Революции
Ulitsa Skorokhodova
Улица Скороходова
Ulitsa Sofie Perovskoi
Улица Софии Перовской
Ulitsa Tolmacheva
Улица Толмачева
Ulitsa Fotievoi
Улица Фотиевой
Ulitsa Fofanovoi
Улица Фофановой
Ulitsa Khalturina
Улица Халтурина
Prospekt Shchorsa
Проспект Щорса

Rizhsky Prospekt
Рижский проспект
Vvedenskaya Ulitsa
Введенская Улица
Furshtadtskaya Ulitsa
Фурштадтская улица
Pochtamtsky Pereulok
Почтамтский переулок
Konnogvardeisky Bulvar
Конногвардейский бульвар
Italyanskaya Ulitsa
Итальянская улица
Troitskaya Ploshchad
Троицкая площадь
Bolshaya Monetnaya Ulitsa
Большая монетная улица
Malaya Konyushennaya Ulitsa
Малая Конюшенная улица
Karavannaya Ulitsa
Караванная Улица
Eletskaya Ulitsa
Елецкая улица
Enotaevskaya Ulitsa
Енотаевская улица
Millionnaya Ulitsa
Миллионная улица
Maly Prospekt (Petrogradskoi Storony)
Малый Проспект (П.С.)

Bridges

Kirovsky Most
Кировский мост
Komsomolsky Most
Комсомольский мост
Most Pestelya
Мост Пестеля
Pionersky Most
Пионерский мост
Most Svobody
Мост свободы

Troitsky Most
Троицкий мост
Kharlamov Most
Харламов мост
Panteleimonovsky Most
Пантелеймоновский мост
Silin Most
Силин мост
Sampsonievsky Most
Сампсониевский мост

Metros

Komsomolskaya
Комсомольская
Krasnogvardeiskaya
Красногвардейская
Ploshchad Mira
Площадь мира

Devyatkino
Девяткино
Novocherkasskaya
Новочеркасская
Sennaya Ploshchad
Сенная площадь

NOTES

FULL SERVICE TRAVEL CENTER

NEVSKIJ PALACE ARCADE
NEVSKY PROSPEKT 57
(812) 314 5086

INTERNATIONAL AIRPORT
(812) 104 3443

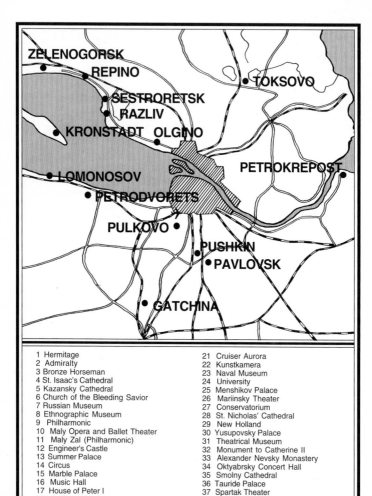

ZELENOGORSK
REPINO
TOKSOVO
SESTRORETSK
RAZLIV
KRONSTADT OLGINO
PETROKREPOST
LOMONOSOV
PETRODVORETS
PULKOVO
PUSHKIN
PAVLOVSK
GATCHINA

1 Hermitage	21 Cruiser Aurora
2 Admiralty	22 Kunstkamera
3 Bronze Horseman	23 Naval Museum
4 St. Isaac's Cathedral	24 University
5 Kazansky Cathedral	25 Menshikov Palace
6 Church of the Bleeding Savior	26 Mariinsky Theater
7 Russian Museum	27 Conservatorium
8 Ethnographic Museum	28 St. Nicholas' Cathedral
9 Philharmonic	29 New Holland
10 Maly Opera and Ballet Theater	30 Yusupovsky Palace
11 Maly Zal (Philharmonic)	31 Theatrical Museum
12 Engineer's Castle	32 Monument to Catherine II
13 Summer Palace	33 Alexander Nevsky Monastery
14 Circus	34 Oktyabrsky Concert Hall
15 Marble Palace	35 Smolny Cathedral
16 Music Hall	36 Tauride Palace
17 House of Peter I	37 Spartak Theater
18 Artillery Museum	38 Jazz Philharmonic Hall
19 Kshesinskaya Mansion	39 Dostoevsky Museum
20 Mosque	40 Pushkin Museum